MICROPROGRAMMING

GUY G. BOULAYE

Department of Mathematics and Computing
University of Rennes, France

Edited by Dr P. A. Beaven

M

© Dunod, 1971

Authorised English language edition, revised and
expanded, of *La Microprogrammation*, first
published 1971 by Dunod, Paris

© English language edition, The Macmillan Press Ltd, 1975

First published 1975 in the United Kingdom by
THE MACMILLAN PRESS LTD
London and Basingstoke
Associated companies in New York Dublin
Melbourne Johannesburg and Madras

SBN 333 17992 7 (hard cover)
333 15079 1 (paper cover)

Typeset in Great Britain by
PREFACE LIMITED
Salisbury, Wilts
and printed in Great Britain by
TINLING (1973) LIMITED
Prescot, Lancs
(a member of the Oxley Printing Group Ltd)

Contents

Foreword

by Douglas Lewin
Professor of Digital Processes
Brunel University

The concept of microprogramming is not new, in fact it was first proposed by Professor M. V. Wilkes in 1951 as a systematic means of designing the hardwired control circuits for digital computers. Since that time the technique has evolved into a recognised logic design philosophy embracing both hardware and software processes.

There are many practical engineering advantages to be gained from using microprogramming techniques, both from the point of view of the manufacturer and the user. Moreover, the availability of micro-programmable machines modifiable by the user and the current research on language emulation and virtual processor structures, have opened up entirely new fields of application.

The development of microprogramming has been primarily due to the impact of integrated circuit technology. The original Wilkes scheme employed a read-only memory, implemented using a ferrite core matrix, to directly generate the control waveforms. The use of semiconductor storage, and in particular writable random access memories, to realise the microprogram control store has allowed the original concept to be refined and developed into a powerful design technique.

Much of the published material concerning the theory and application of microprogramming is to be found scattered throughout journals and conference proceedings, and hence is difficult for the computer engineer to acquire. Professor Guy Boulaye's book has now remedied this situation and presents a clear account of the fundamental principles of the subject coupled with a critical survey of established practice and current research. A particular feature of the book is the good introduction it offers to the theoretical methods of describing and minimising microprogram sequences. This book should be prescribed reading for anyone concerned with the design and application of digital computer systems.

The original text was published in France and is indicative of the high level of computer technology in that country and Europe generally. Tribute must also be paid to Dr Paul Beaven's excellent editorship without which the English edition would not have been possible.

Notation and Symbols

If R designates a store, a register, a bus, etc. then

(1) R $[i,j]$, with $[i,j] \subset Z$ (Z being the set of the integers) designates the sub-store of bits i to j inclusively, the sub-register of i to j, the sub-bus of the wires i to j, etc. For R$[i,i]$, we shall simply use R$[i]$.

(2) [R] designates the content of R.

(3) The arrow →indicates a transfer.

Examples

R[0,15] : if R is a register, R[0,15] designates the bits 0 to 15 inclusive.

M[255] : if M is a store, M[255] is the cell whose address is 255.

M[(R[0,15])] designates the cell whose address is found in R[0,15]

M[(M[255])] is an indirect addressing via cell 255

[(M[255] [4]) designates the content of bit 4 of location 255

If there is no ambiguity, the parentheses will be omitted, for example

$$R1[-1,15] \longrightarrow R2[0,16]$$

This permits the simple representation of linked transfers. For example

$$IC \longrightarrow A \longrightarrow R \text{ replaces (IC)} \longrightarrow A; (A) \longrightarrow R$$

in the case of a transfer of the content of register IC into register R via the bus A. Similarly, R$[k]$ can be replaced by Rk (for example, locally in a formula). Generally, however R1 and R2 will designate two different registers and not bits 1 and 2 of the same register R.

We shall even extend this notation to non-physical elements. For example, INST[4,5] will designate bits 4 and 5 of the instruction word. Or indeed, writing

$$(R[(INST[4,5])]) \longrightarrow M[(INST[8,15])]$$

indicates that the content of register R, whose address is indicated in bits 4 and 5 of the current instruction is transferred into the memory address indicated in bits 8 and 15 of the same instruction word.

Notation such as INST[OP] designating the OP part of the word INST will also be used.

Operator Symbols
Arithmetic addition: +
Logical union bit-to-bit: V or + (the OR operator)
Logical intersection bit-to-bit: ∧ or · (the AND operator)
Logical disjunction bit-to-bit: + (the 'exclusive-OR' operator)

Commands
Notation x/M indicates that the command x is applied to the module M.

  If M is a memory, then the command may be Read/M . . .
  For a counter IC, ADV/IC or RESET/IC
  For a register R , Load/R

We shall denote A & B as the set of AND gates controlling the transfer from A to B. If the command for A & B is OP (for OPEN), then the command may be OP/A & B.

Example

    OP/R[(INST [S])] & B

Also, calling EN the enable signal of a selection command, we shall find, for example

    EN/R [⟨address⟩] Sel B

Graphical Conventions for Operators
OR Gate

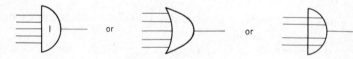

AND Gate

For every logic network for which there is no special convention

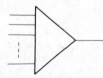

Inverter

$$x \;\triangleright\!\!\circ\; \bar{x}$$

1 The Concept of Control in a Stored Program Computer: Microprogramming

1.1 The Instruction

A computer program is made up of instructions which direct a sequence of processing operations. These operations follow one after the other without external intervention and hence the epithet 'automatic' is frequently applied to computers. The job of organising the automatic flow of instructions is vital to the computer's operation hence a special unit within the computer – the control unit – is used to perform this function.

Inside the computer an instruction is represented as a fixed length boolean vector (the instruction word) which for the purposes of interpretation by the control unit is usually broken down into several parts. These parts are generally of fixed length and occupy a fixed position in the instruction word. As a rule the significance of the various parts that make up the instruction word arises from the fact that an instruction includes the following information

(a) an operation code, called the 'Op code',

(b) information about the operands and the result; generally these are the operand addresses and the result address;

(c) an indication of the next address in the program sequence;

(d) special bits indicating indexing, memory protection, parity, etc.

Coding all the above information into the instruction word would require rather a large number of bits and a useful economy is achieved by making certain addresses implicit.

Next Instruction A useful and not very restricting procedure is to place the linear sequence of program instructions in successive addresses of the memory. Hence with the exception of a program jump, the address of the next instruction becomes a matter of course and its detailed specification in the instruction word becomes unnecessary. At each given moment in time the control unit must know the current point that has been reached in the execution of the program, this point being retained by the *instruction counter* which stores the address of the instruction in hand. The term instruction counter is used because its updating is achieved by incrementation.

Operands and Results Basically for operations involving two operands, three addresses are necessary (that is, addresses for the two operands and the result). In general, it is not too restricting to use a common address for both the result and one of the two operands. Operations on the contents of registers (addition, subtraction, etc.) are often of this type. Moreover, since the number of registers in a machine is very small (when compared with the number of words in the memory), very few bits of the instruction word are required for register addressing. Hence the richness of the instruction repertoire is often developed to the benefit of operations between registers, and instructions involving operands in the store become limited to transfers between register and store.

Clearly these simplifications of the operating structure must be paid for by the imposition of certain programming constraints. Ideally the problem being solved by the program should lend itself to such treatment and this is frequently the case in iterative problems of a scientific nature, in which only a few intermediate results need be retained between successive steps of the calculation. Where this is the case the central registers that contain the intermediate results can be considered as the top (most frequently accessed) level of the storage hierarchy.

In order to make even more economies in the instruction coding, one of the two operands can be made implicit. For example in loading or storage operations the source or destination of a data transfer can be made implicit in the instruction itself. In this case the implicit register is referred to as the accumulator and a good example is the 'load accumulator' type of instruction.

1.2 Signals and Information in a Computer

In a computer the information is presented in the form of binary numbers and a component capable of memorising these numbers must have two stable states. One of these states is by convention given the value 0, the other the value 1.

When the information is to be rapidly transmitted, modified, assembled, etc., it is translated into physical terms in the form of electrical signals. These signals will have two possible values, which usually correspond to the absence or presence of electrical activity.

Transmitting an item of information from A to B involves linking A to B by a conducting path. Given that the link from A to B may be achieved, it is important to have a method of controlling the information flow, that is, it should be possible to break the link when it

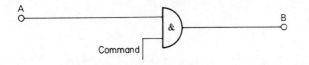

Figure 1.1

is not required. To provide the control an AND operator (Figure 1.1) is inserted between A and B, where the control input takes the form of a command signal (called a micro-command in the next section). If the command has the value 1, A and B take the same logical value. Alternatively if the command is 0, A is not passed on to B and in fact a 0 is transmitted. As the link between A and B may be opened or closed the name GATE is given to the AND operator.

When B can receive information coming from one of several sources A, A′, A″, . . . the outputs of the command gates of links AB, A′B, A″B are combined using an OR operator (figure 1.2). Notice that it is only possible for a single source of information to be connected to B at a given time (that is, only one command signal may have the value 1).

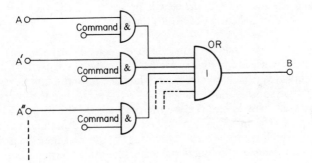

Figure 1.2

If the information at the points A and B is to take the form of a binary vector rather than a single bit, a multiplicity of gates is used as shown in figure 1.3.

The command signal is in effect a sampling pulse and similarly a non-0 signal arriving at B also takes the form of a pulse.

We have just seen how to select and guide an item of information. However this information is transient, and having reached its destination it must be memorised in a register. The wires arriving at this register are permanent and therefore signals are continually present at the register input. When these signals are indicative of the information

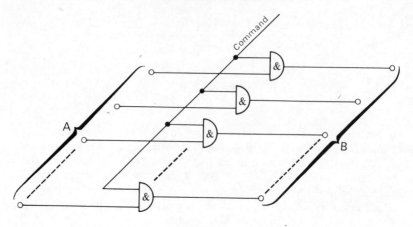

Figure 1.3

sent, a control input to the register is pulsed and the information on the signal wires is recorded in the register itself.

Usually a 0 command forbids recording. Conversely, when the command has the value 1, the signals present on the input wires of the register are recorded (or *loaded*) into the register.

Synchronisation   Load commands are generally synchronised by gating them with a common periodic *clock signal* (figure 1.4). In the time interval T_1, the stored register values are constant, and new values cannot be established until the interval T_2. Again, once the interval T_2 is terminated, new values replace the old ones on the output wires of the registers. The interval T_1 must be of sufficient duration to allow all functions which are to be recorded during T_2 to reach their final values. In fact, for simple combinational gate circuits a certain time must elapse before an input can propagate through to establish the output at its correct new value. This interval of time, allowing for a safety margin, must be less than T_1. The new value is memorised during T_2, and can in turn serve, during the following T_1 interval, to produce new function values that will be memorised during the next clock pulse. The combination of the intervals T_1 and T_2 is called a *cycle*.

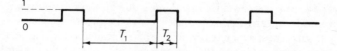

Figure 1.4

The technique of clock synchronisation is not restricted to the loading command and in practice all register commands (shifts, resets, etc.) are controlled in this way.

It should be noted that if the clock signal is suppressed, the content of the registers is fixed for as long as the interruption persists. Operation is therefore stopped, and so this technique provides a means of delaying a particular part of a circuit (which may be reactivated when appropriate conditions outside the circuit are satisfied).

1.3 Flow of an Instruction – Control Unit

Figure 1.5 shows the layout of a small computer. The register P, in conjunction with the accumulator ACC, allows the multiply or divide functions to be performed by the arithmetic and logic unit (the ALU).

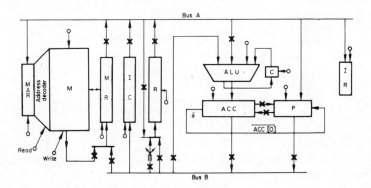

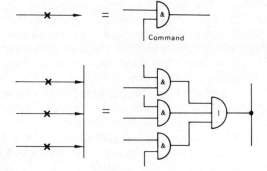

Figure 1.5

The main store M, which will be assumed to have a 'destructive read', operates in the following manner.

READ   At the initiation of this command the memory address register (MAR) contains the address of the word to be read from the memory. When the read is complete the stored word output by the memory is transferred to the register MR.

Since we have assumed a destructive read the very action of reading a particular word in memory will have destroyed the contents of that word. Hence the stored information just erased must be once again rewritten and this is achieved using the WRITE command without changing the contents of MAR or MR.

WRITE   Prior to writing the addressed word is filled with zeros by a read operation, though in this case the information emerging from the store is not transferred to the register MR. With this preparation completed the writing operation is carried out as above.

MAR — memory address register
M   — memory
MR   — memory register
IC   — instruction counter
R   — a register
P   — a register
ALU — arithmetic and logic unit (purely combinational)
ACC — accumulator—output register of ALU
C   — addition carry store
IR   — instruction register

We shall assume (see table 1.1) that a reading or writing operation occupies three clock cycles.

Having discussed the destructive nature of the memory READ operation, it is important to stress that the contents of a register are not so vulnerable and may be read without causing mutilation. (Registers are usually built using the master—slave technique.)

To the programmer an instruction appears to be the smallest distinguishable action in the functioning of a computer. In fact this rather global view of an instruction conceals an operation which has several successive steps, and these involve much more elementary functions internal to the computer.

As an example consider the computer shown in figure 1.5 and suppose that an addition instruction is to add the contents of R and ACC, and place the result in R. When the instruction begins, only the address contained in the instruction counter IC is known. The sequence of operations to be performed, grouped into those which can be done during the same cycle, is shown in table 1.1. The *Commands* column shows the 'active' commands and it is assumed that these signals have the value 1; the commands not mentioned are taken to be 0. In a given

Table 1.1

Cycle	Description	Commands
0	IC → A → MAR; A → ALU; +1/ALU	OP/IC & A OP/A & ALU +1/ALU Load/ACC Load/MAR
	Explanation: the contents of IC are simultaneously transmitted to the MAR and to the ALU, via bus A. In the ALU, 1 is added to (IC) and thus ACC will contain, except in the case of a conditional jump, the address of the next instruction. IC thus arrives in the ALU via one of the two arrival connections for operands. It is therefore necessary to ensure that 0 arrives via the other connection. (The +1 is assumed to be internal to the ALU.) The 0 inputs to the ALU are achieved by closing the gates bringing information carried via bus B.	
	In addition it is very important to avoid losing the original contents of ACC and hence provision is made for retaining (ACC) in a convenient register, for example in IC.	OP/ACC & B Load/IC
	ACC → B → IC	
1	Read/M; ACC → B → IC	Read/M OP/ACC & B Load/IC
	Explanation: as the address register of the store M was loaded during cycle 0 a read in memory M is now initiated. Simultaneously the content of ACC (that is the address of the next instruction) is transmitted to the IC. At the same time the content of IC, (the original ACC value) is returned to the ACC. This is done via the ALU in which (IC) is in fact added to zero	OP/IC & A OP/A & ALU +/ALU Load/ACC
	IC → A → ALU → ACC	
2	Read/M	Read/M
	Explanation: the read cycle continues. (*Note*: it is assumed that a read operation occupies three cycles.)	
3	M[MAR] → MR	Read/M OP/M & MR Load/MR
	Explanation: third and last read cycle. The word output by the memory must be loaded into register MR.	

Table 1.1 (*continued*)

Cycle	Description	Commands
4	MR → A → IR; write/M	OP/MR & A
		Load/IR
	Explanation: at the end of the read cycle the instruction is located in the MR and it is sent via bus A into register IR where it will be analysed by the control unit in subsequent cycles. Simultaneously the instruction is rewritten in its original place in store to compensate for the destructive reading operation.	Write/M
	(*Note*: the instruction address is still present in the MAR.)	
5	Write/M	Write/M
	the rewriting continues.	
6	Write/M	Write/M
	the rewriting continues.	
7	R → A → ALU; ACC → B → ALU; +/ALU	OP/R & A
		OP/A & ALU
	Explanation: the contents of R and ACC are directed to the ALU, where they are added together. The result is recorded in ACC.	OP/ACC & B
		OP/B & ALU
		+/ALU
		Load/ACC
8	ACC → B → R	OP/ACC & B
		OP/B & R
	Explanation: the result of the addition is sent into R via B. The instruction is terminated.	Load/R

cycle, the active commands give the result described in the *Description* column.

In the absence of any incident (for example, an overflow in the above addition), the computer moves on to the next instruction and it should be noticed that regardless of instruction type, this next instruction will perform the same first seven steps as for the addition. These seven steps constitute what is called *the fetch phase*, in the course of which the instruction is extracted from the memory and placed in the instruction register IR.

During the following cycles (in this case cycles 7 and 8), an operation will take place that is specific to each instruction. These cycles are said to constitute the *execution phase*. In order to increase computing speed, it is sometimes possible to make the two phases overlap. Thus, in our example, the execution could have begun from cycle 5 since this execution does not affect registers MAR and MR and therefore the rewriting can continue in an independent fashion. In this case two cycles can be saved.

Control Unit   The above example shows us that during each cycle certain commands take the value 1 while others are kept at 0. As already indicated the set of commands is generated by a special unit called the *control unit*. Thus the part of the computer shown in figure 1.5 is designated the *execution network*; the relationships between the execution network and its control unit being outlined in figure 1.6.

At each cycle, the control unit CU emits commands destined for the execution network (write/M, load/ACC, OP/MR & A, etc.); to be more precise, at each cycle the CU transmits on the wire corresponding to each command the correct value, 0 or 1, depending on whether the command must be active or not during that cycle.

From time to time the CU needs an instruction, which will be held in the IR. Also during some instructions the CU uses additional information, generally called the *condition code* CC, concerning the status of the execution network (for example, value of a carry, the sign of the last result, etc.).

In order to know where it is in the processing of the instruction in hand, the CU has a number of 'status bits' which are constantly updated to represent the current state of the instruction. The form of these status bits depends on the structure of the CU itself. Also for each step in the execution of an instruction, the CU transmits a boolean command vector to the execution network. We will regard this vector as

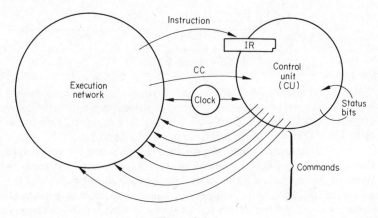

Figure 1.6

a word, the command word. At each cycle the CU must therefore generate a control word and update its own status bits.

There are two extreme types of realisation of the control unit.

(a) Either the control word can be produced at each cycle: this is the *wired solution*. The status bits are generally small counters and their updating is done by advancement, resetting or initialisation.

(b) Or the control words can be pre-recorded in a special store, called the *command store*, and at each cycle the necessary word can be accessed. The status bits are now a specification of the next control word to be used, most often by indicating a modification of the current address in the command store. This is the *microprogrammed* solution.

The indication of the next word forms part of the word read in the command store; we will call this the 'next address' part.

Whether it is wired or microprogrammed, the control unit organises the operation sequence shown in the following flowchart.

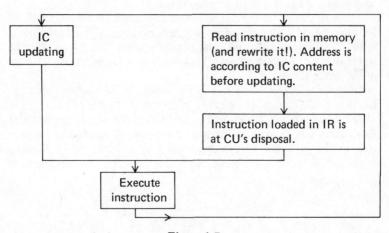

Figure 1.7

Status Information in a Control Unit   In order to synthesise a control unit, the sequences of control words that it must generate need to be established. This can be done by constructing a table (1.2) similar to table 1.1 but with an additional column for CU status bits.

For the same execution network, the possible control realisations vary only in the CU status bits column. This column in fact contains information for updating the status bits themselves. For example, for a wired control unit, there will be commands for controlling the small counters which provide status information for the CU (see reference 4, pp. 269–76).

Table 1.2

Cycle	Description–Explanation	Commands	CU status bits
0	.	.	.
1	.	.	.
.	.	.	.
.	.	.	.
.	.	.	.

For a microprogrammed control unit, the status column will contain commands such as: Adv/C MAR or RESET/C MAR least significant bits, in which C MAR is the address register of the store containing the microprograms (see section 1.8).

Microinstruction   This is a word contained in the command store of a microprogrammed control unit; it therefore consists of a command word and the next address (which points towards the next micro-instruction). We shall of course return to consider a microinstruction in more detail.

Microcommands   These are what we have referred to hitherto as commands; they are represented by a signal, carried by a particular wire to a well-defined destination. Some examples are

(a) for a counter; the advance microcommand (and corresponding wire), the reset-to-zero microcommand (and its wire), etc.
(b) for the main store; the read and write microcommands (and their wires).

1.4 Microprograms

Just as a coherent sequence of instructions, contributing to an operation, is called a program, so a coherent sequence of microinstructions, for example corresponding to a fetch phase or to the execution of an instruction, will be called a microprogram. As in a program, a microprogram ends by pointing towards the start address of the next microprogram. The structure of the set of microprograms contained in a microprogrammed control unit is indicated in the flowchart of figure 1.7. Strictly the execution box contains a group of execution modules corresponding to the required instruction set. At the end of the fetch phase a branch is made towards the execution module of the current instruction.

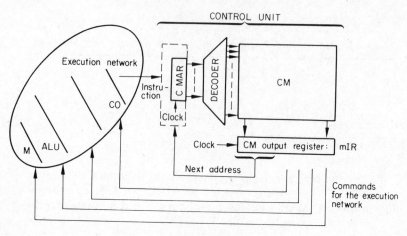

Figure 1.8

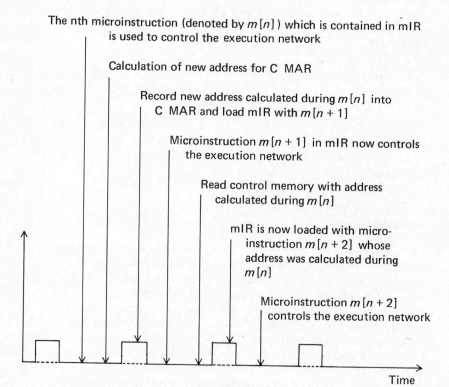

The nth microinstruction (denoted by $m[n]$) which is contained in mIR is used to control the execution network

Calculation of new address for C MAR

Record new address calculated during $m[n]$ into C MAR and load mIR with $m[n+1]$

Microinstruction $m[n+1]$ in mIR now controls the execution network

Read control memory with address calculated during $m[n]$

mIR is now loaded with microinstruction $m[n+2]$ whose address was calculated during $m[n]$

Microinstruction $m[n+2]$ controls the execution network

Time

Figure 1.9

1.5 Functioning of the Microprogrammed Control Unit

The microinstruction words that make up the various microprograms are stored in a special memory, a simplified block diagram of which is shown in figure 1.8. The address register MAR C contains the address of the word to be extracted. A decoder decodes this address and indicates which of the words is to be read. The contents of the chosen word are placed in the output register or microinstruction register mIR. The microinstruction stored in mIR during a given cycle controls the execution circuits during that cycle.

As described, the memory need only provide read-only storage (that is, it is non-writable). The timing of the control memory is such that a read takes one clock cycle at the end of which the mIR contains the new microinstruction (see figure 1.9).

The main point to be noted is that during the course of cycle n, the microinstruction in hand does not indicate the next microinstruction but the next but one.

The command for loading into mIR is simply the clock signal and at the end of each cycle a new microinstruction which will control the circuits during the next cycle is loaded into mIR. It is this mechanism that constitutes the automatic nature of the computer.

1.6 Microinstruction Fields

The microinstruction word is divided into sub-words called *fields*.

Setting aside its next address part, the microinstruction word defines the behaviour of the components of the execution network during the cycle in which this microinstruction is controlling the machine. The simplest method of using this word is to partition the machine into functionally independent regions, and to allocate a field of the microinstruction word for each region.

Example of a Field   In controlling the instruction counter, we need the following facilities: incrementation, resetting to zero, loading, leaving unchanged. These are four mutually exclusive contingencies and therefore two bits are sufficient to code this field. For example

IC field value	Meaning
01	increment
10	reset to zero
11	load
00	leave unchanged

Using these two bits a decoder can generate the three microcommands

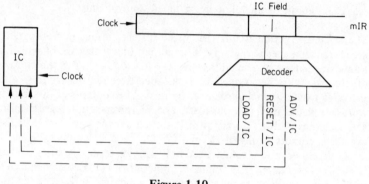

Figure 1.10

ADV/IC, RESET/IC and LOAD/IC. (See figure 1.10, which indicates the links between the mIR field and the corresponding microcommands.)

1.7 Micro-orders

A micro-order is the content of a field and typical examples include

OP/IC & A   READ/M   WRITE/M   ADV/IC   +/ALU

The example in section 1.6 shows the link between the micro-order and microcommand: the microcommands are obtained by decoding the micro-orders. Sometimes coding, which tends to economise on the bits in the command memory, is unnecessary. Let us consider for example the main store field M. Here two commands must be generated, and including the no-operation state, this means that the three contingencies must be coded using a two-bit field. In terms of decoding it is simplest to provide one bit for WRITE/M and one for READ/M. (Value 11 is forbidden while value 00 translates as no active command, that is, the no-operation state.)

1.8 Other Fields

There are other fields besides those corresponding either to the control of operators (for example, READ/M, +/ALU) or to the organisation of the transfers of information (for example, OP/R & B). Some examples are given below.

Next Address Part   The next microinstruction must be designated by its address. The problem is relatively complicated because microprograms sometimes have common parts. The fetch phase, for example, is common to all the instructions. Alternatively if the SIN function were provided as an instruction, it would probably use the multiplication microprogram as a subroutine.

Delay Function   This function indicates when the transition to the next microinstruction is to be made (see section 1.3). Although this is a complex problem and we shall be returning to it in more detail in later chapters, it is worth pointing out at this stage that a simple solution is obtained by making all microinstructions last for the same period of time. In this case there is no problem of timing and although this is the simplest solution, it is not very often the most practical one.

In cases where the transition to the next microinstruction is made at the end of a variable interval of time, this must be explicitly indicated using the delay function part of the microinstruction word.

Special Bits   These include check bits or bits whose interpretation is a function of the microinstruction, for example, parity bits, etc.

1.9 Concept of Addressing in the Command Memory

The address register of the command memory drives an address decoder, which in turn provides the signals selecting the corresponding word in the command memory. The word is extracted and recorded in the output register mIR (figure 1.11).

Let us imagine a computer having 15 instructions $I1, I2, \ldots I15$ with an operation code of four bits. Suppose also that no instruction has the code 0000. Each instruction must be implemented by a set of microinstructions. A simple means of doing this is to divide the command memory into 15 + 1 pages, so that the page number is given by the operation code. It is a simple matter to place the fetch microprogram in page 0 so that at the end of the execution microprogram of each instruction one has only to reset the address register to zero.

At the end of the fetch microprogram, the first instruction of the appropriate execution microprogram must be chosen. This is done by loading the most-significant C MAR bits with the Op code and by re-setting the least-significant bits to zero. The microprogram will thus begin in the first word of the corresponding page. Within a page the procedure is conveniently advanced by incrementation of the least-significant bits of the C MAR.

Leaving aside the jump within microprograms the device as presented will function correctly provided that the updating of the C MAR during the microinstruction N involved microinstruction $N+2$. For example, this assumes that the instruction is available, and that its

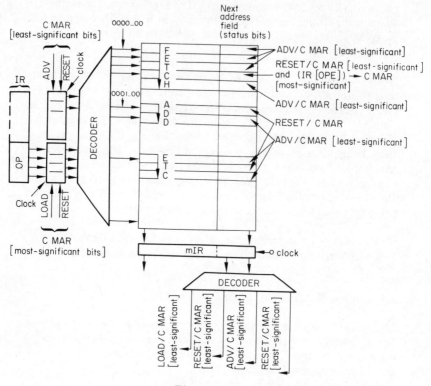

Figure 1.11

Op code part can be loaded into C MAR, during the penultimate cycle of the fetch phase.

To summarise: in the penultimate cycle of the fetch phase

   RESET/C MAR [least significant]

and

   (IR[OP]) ———→ C MAR [most significant]

In the penultimate cycle of an execution phase.

   RESET/C MAR [all bits]

This description is oversimplified, and in practice addressing is more complicated; however the idea remains the same. Hence we can now define a microprogrammed computer as a computer in which the instructions are interpreted as calls on routines recorded in a special store.

1.10 Problems Posed by the Designation of the Next Microinstruction

These problems result principally from trying either to reduce the size of the address part in the microinstruction word, or to minimise the total number of words of the command memory. The outcome is that the microprograms are considerably interleaved, resulting in numerous switches. Consequently the next address part does not generally indicate a single following address but several, from which a selection must be made from a number of possible alternatives. (In order to minimise execution times, the mechanism governing this choice is usually 'hard-wired'.) The choice frequently involves tests on previous results or tests performed by hard-wired circuits and recorded in the condition flip—flops. Alternatively the next address might be subject to a special bit of the operation code.

Another problem occurs when two cycles of the read-only store elapse between the loading of the control memory address register and the moment when the corresponding microinstruction controls the execution circuits. This lag is not important for a 'jump-free' sequence of microinstructions as it is sufficient to load the address register at time $t - 2$, with the address of the microinstruction needed at time t. The problem occurs when in cycle t, the microinstruction in course of execution indicates a branch address conditioned by the result of a test carried out in time t.

This address cannot therefore be written into the address register before time t and the corresponding microinstruction must be executed at $t + 2$: nothing is done during time $t + 1$ and therefore a cycle has been lost. What is more, if many conditional branches are made, numerous cycles will be lost as a consequence.

1.11 Dimensions of Microcommand Stores

Small computers of the order of 4000 to 30 000 bits (for example, the Elbit-100 or the Multi-8)

> k times 256 words of 16 bits ($k = 1,2,3,4$)

Medium and large scale computers

> k times 1024 words of 50—100 bits ($k = 1,2,3 \ldots 8$)

in other words, of the order of 100 000 to 500 000 bits.

This first chapter provides a résumé of the subject. Many of the ideas that have been introduced will be considered in more detail in subsequent chapters.

2 Control Storage Technology

2.1 A Model of the Control Store

The model of the control store shown in figure 2.1 has two important attributes. First the memory cycle time is the same as that of the registers, and second, once the instruction repertoire is fixed and the microprograms written, the memory contents need never be modified. It follows from these attributes that a read-only memory is quite adequate, particularly since the special technology involved enables the necessarily high operating speeds (memory cycle = clock cycle) to be attained.

A two-dimensional arrangement is the one most often used because it is well suited to memories with small numbers of long words (this

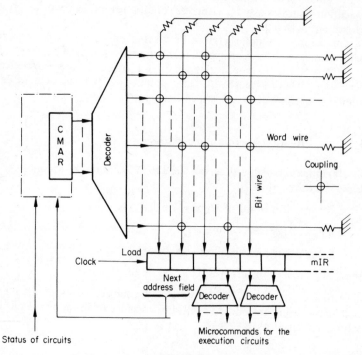

Figure 2.1

being the case with the microprograms envisaged here), and also because this configuration gives very fast access times.

After decoding the C MAR register the decoder transmits a 1 to the selected word wire. When bit i of the selected word is 1, a coupling transmits the 1 present on the word wire along the ith bit wire. This signal serves as input for the mIR $[i]$ cell. When the selected word is 0 at position i, no coupling takes place, and thus we say that 'only the 1s are realised'.

Since the bit wire is common to all words, the coupling technology must be such that the input to mIR $[i]$ is formed by the logical OR of all word wires having a 1 in ith position.

Three types of coupling exist, and we shall review these in turn; they are resistive (including semiconductors), electromagnetic, and capacitive. (To avoid ambiguity in the definition of voltages it will be assumed that all word and bit wires are connected to earth potential via high impedances as shown in figure 2.1.)

2.2 Resistive Coupling

2.2.1 Coupling by Diodes

This is the most direct method (see figure 2.2a). Let us assume there is a positive signal on a word wire, representing a 1. At those points where

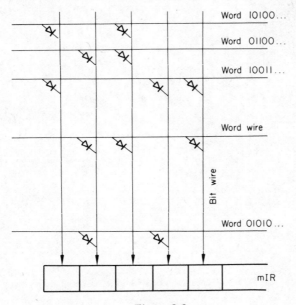

Figure 2.2a

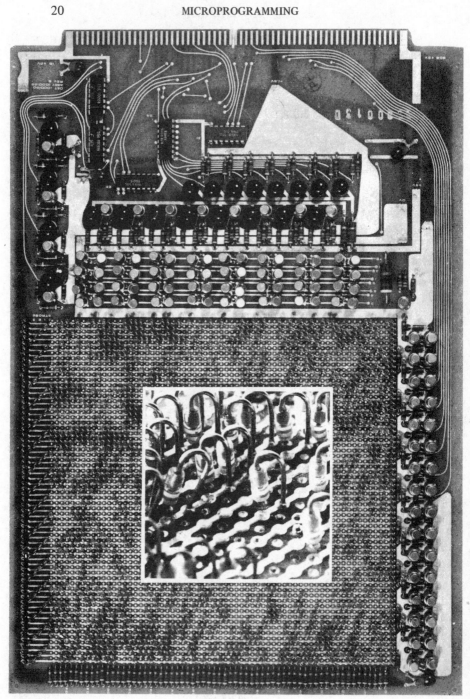

Figure 2.2b

the stored word contains a 1, a diode is placed to transmit the word signal to the input of the corresponding cell in the microinstruction register mIR. Where no diode exists, the signal is not transmitted and a 0 will be recorded in the mIR cell.

Figure 2.2b shows an example of a read-only memory using diodes.

2.2.2 Coupling by Resistors

As shown in figure 2.3, the coupling can be made using resistors. Often these components are formed by vacuum deposition; a good example can be found in the Elbit-100 computer.

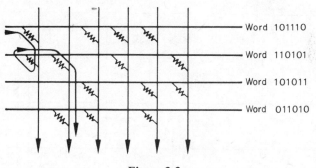

Figure 2.3

Although the simplicity of the resistive storage array keeps the cost of stored information to a modest level, it is important to take account of the unwanted couplings that inevitably exist. Let us suppose that the first word wire of figure 2.3 is selected. A current now flows dividing itself among the various resistors, and since, unlike diodes, resistors permit current to flow in either direction, the current can follow quite complicated routes. Thus a small current flows in the second bit wire even though the selected word has a 0 in this position. It is true that the current is about three times weaker than that for a 1, but nevertheless as it is non-zero the electronic detection devices which monitor this current need to be rather more sophisticated than in the case of diode coupling.

2.2.3 Coupling by Transistor

Coupling between word and bit wires can also be achieved by feeding the signal present on the selected word wire to the base of a transistor, thus causing it to conduct (see figures 2.4a and b).

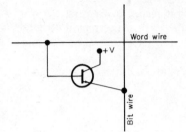

(a)

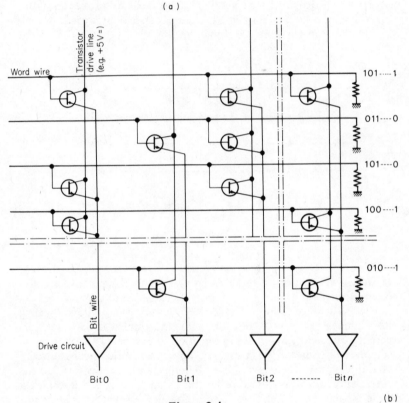

(b)

Figure 2.4

Compared with diodes, transistors offer the advantage of isolating the circuits of the word wires from those of the bit wires. This simplifies the design of the drive circuits, allowing long words and facilitating faster operating speeds.

A solution of this type has been adopted for the Illiac IV computer, whose read-only store has a capacity of 720 words of 280 bits and a cycle time of 50 nanoseconds.

2.3 Electromagnetic Coupling

2.3.1 Principles of Operation

In essence a current in the word wire induces a voltage in the bit wire, the coupling being obtained with the aid of a magnetic circuit. In practice there are three basic forms of magnetic coupling.

(a) A magnetic circuit by bit (that is, by memory point at the intersection of the word and bit wires). Here permanent 'writing' is obtained by placing a magnetic circuit at those points of the matrix which must generate a 1 (figure 2.5a). The required pattern of toroidal cores is usually obtained by manufacturing the full matrix and destroying (or suppressing) those toroids corresponding to a 0.

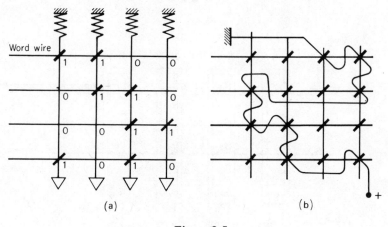

Figure 2.5

When the magnetic material has a rectangular hysteresis loop the toroids can also be placed in all positions, but the coupling of the 0s is made inoperative by means of a polarisation wire which saturates the corresponding magnetic circuits (figure 2.5b). Unfortunately, between cycles the toroids must be reset, since in this case it is the change of state of the toroids which provides a readable pulse. This can be done by means of a wire linking all the toroids.

It should be appreciated that this technique is only of value for experimental work or at the stage of prototype studies. It is better to use toroids made from a linear material without excessive hysteresis as this avoids the problems of resetting.

(b) A magnetic circuit by word (figure 2.6)
(c) A magnetic circuit by bit position (figure 2.7)

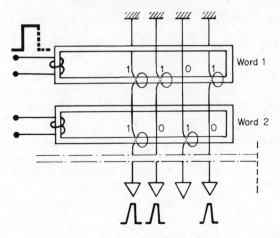

Figure 2.6

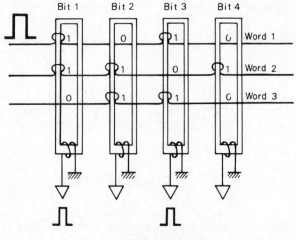

Figure 2.7

Since in general the number of words is far greater than the number of bits per word, technique (c) is usually more difficult to implement than technique (b).

2.3.2 Magnetic Bar Memory

This is an example of a technology using the one magnetic circuit per bit configuration. In this case a magnetic material is chosen which has no hysteresis and a high coefficient of magnetic permeability. In figure 2.8 the word wire either surrounds or by-passes the bar,

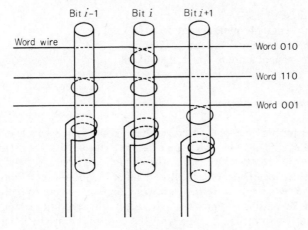

Figure 2.8

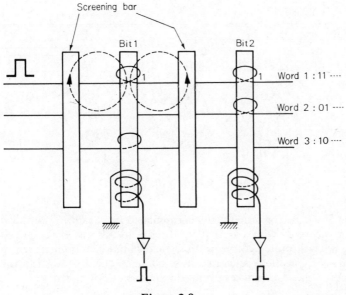

Figure 2.9

depending on whether the stored bit is a 1 or 0. A turn of the word wire forms the primary of a transformer with the bar constituting the magnetic circuit and a few turns forming the secondary. Using this arrangement the detection of a 1 (or 0) is made by detecting the presence (or absence) of a signal induced in the secondary winding. In order to enclose the magnetic circuit and to suppress unwanted couplings, a third screening bar is often inserted between adjacent bars (figure 2.9).

Typical dimensions
>   Bar: length 40 mm, diameter 2.5 mm
>   Threading wire diameter: 15/100 mm
>   (Permanent store of the Bull M-40 computer)

2.3.3 Transformer Memory

The transformer memory described here is a further example of a
magnetic circuit per bit. This type of store (figure 2.10) is constructed
using ferrite cores which again have high permeability and low
hysteresis characteristics. Each bit column of the matrix representation
is replaced by a single core: the word wire looping the core to represent
a 1 and by-passing to provide a 0. As in the previous example a
transformer is formed, this time with the core as the magnetic circuit,
and again a secondary winding is used to detect the presence or absence
of a 1.

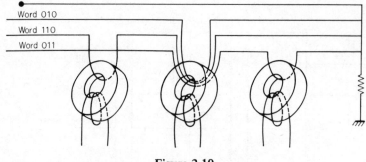

Word 010
Word 110
Word 011

Figure 2.10

The arrays of cores are usually encapsulated in a flexible resin which
in turn is covered with a layer of hard resin. In this way the cores and
wiring are well protected against shock and vibration, but the increased
capacitive connection between the word lines due to the dielectric
constant of the resin reduces the maximum operating frequency.

Typical dimensions
>   The outside core diameter is usually in the order of 4—5 mm for
>   wires of 0.1 mm diameter, but in some cases outside diameters as
>   large as 20 mm have been used.
>   (This form of coupling has been used for the read-only store of
>   the Interdata 4 computer which has 512 words of bits and a 400
>   ns cycle time.)

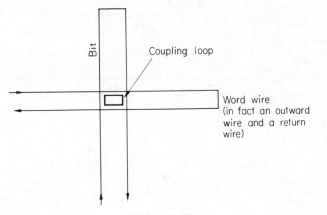

Figure 2.11

2.3.4 *Loop Coupling*

This is an example of a magnetic circuit by bit. The principle is shown in figure 2.11 where two long narrow rectangular loops of wire are placed in two parallel planes very close to one another so that the loops are at right angles. In this configuration the inductive coupling between these two loops is practically zero and sending a current pulse along one loop will not give rise to any induced voltage in the other. The first loop is called the interrogation loop and the second the read loop.

If however we place a short-circuited turn, called a coupling loop, on the small area common to the two main loops, an eddy current is induced in the coupling loop and the flux linkage thus established provides a coupling between the interrogation and the read loops. A command store can be made by creating a parallel network of interrogation loops which are crossed at right-angles by a network of reading loops, with suitably positioned coupling loops. In practice the construction of this form of memory is simplified by placing coupling loops in all positions and then cutting those loops where 0 is required.

Typical dimensions
    Reading and interrogation loops use wire of 0.4 mm diameter
    Width of loops 2.5 mm
    Distance between interrogation and read loops 15/100 mm

2.4 Capacitive Coupling

A capacitor can be used as a coupling element as shown in figure 2.12. Selection consists of sending a pulse along the chosen word line, this pulse being transmitted at those points where the capacitors are

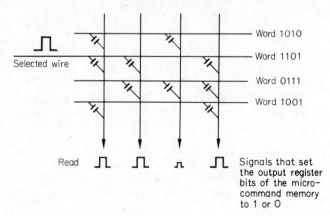

Figure 2.12

located, that is, where the word contains a 1. As an example to show how technologists try to improve manufacture, operating speeds, component costs and achieve a good packing density, we shall consider the solution used by IBM for the 360-30 computer (figure 2.13).

The word and bit wires are made from very flat conductors having a width of about 1 mm and a thickness of 0.05 mm. The planar assemblies of word and bit wires are placed one on top of the other with a very small inter-plane gap. By arranging the direction of the conductors in the two planes to be at right-angles, relatively large capacitances are created at the intersections where bit and word conductors cross over one another.

Capacitive coupling is prevented at those points where a zero is to be stored by inserting an electrostatic screen (a metallic surface connected

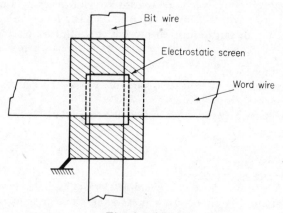

Figure 2.13

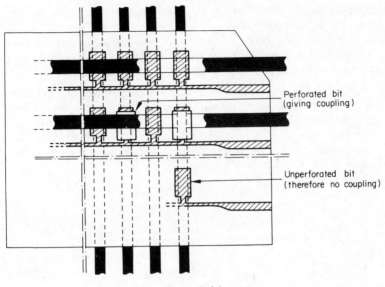

Perforated bit
(giving coupling)

Unperforated bit
(therefore no coupling)

Figure 2.14

to a constant potential, usually earth) between the two conducting surfaces. In fact it proves more practicable to provide a screen at every junction and to destroy it wherever a coupling is required. In the IBM memory these screens are supported by light strong card, similar to the punched cards used in data processing. The screens are placed over the intersections of the columns and rows (figure 2.14). The 'holes', that is, the 1 bits, can be punched out by means of a normal card-punch, thus avoiding manual errors.

2.5 Integrated Circuit Command Stores

As can be seen from the previous examples the command store is a very regular network. It thus lends itself to large scale integration (LSI). The advantages are the same as for semiconductor integrated circuits: reliability, compact construction, low power consumption, high operating speed and compatability with other associated semiconductor circuits (decoders, registers, etc). As a result, semiconductor integrated command memories are frequently superior to other ROM techniques. It is advantageous to include the address decoding network in the integrated circuit chip since this ensures faster operating speeds and reduces the number of pin connections to the integrated circuit. The words of these memory modules are generally short and are often only a single bit wide. For example, modules are frequently made containing

256 1-bit words. Thus to provide 256 n-bit words, n such modules would be required side by side.

During the manufacture of integrated memories a coupling semiconductor is first produced at each array point. Subsequently, the desired pattern of 0s and 1s may be established by one of two techniques.

Masking In the earlier stages of manufacture, the coupling semiconductor is formed, but not linked to the bit wire (figure 2.15). Then in a final production phase, only those connections that correspond to a 1 are made by means of a relatively cheap purpose-made mask (the masks used for the earlier phases of manufacture having a standardised format).

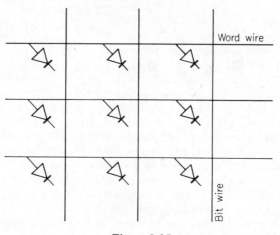

Figure 2.15

Fusible Links Using this techique, the couplings are again established at all matrix points and those corresponding to 0s are subsequently broken. This is done by using a fusible aluminium wire connection (figure 2.16) with a narrow portion such that a sufficiently strong current can break the connection without damaging the rest of the circuit. The fusing current is usually obtained by discharging a capacitor.

Of the two methods of semiconductor coupling, the masking technique is more expensive since a specific mask is involved for each application, but at present it seems to be the more reliable.

The name PROM, for Programmable Read-Only Memory, is often given to this type of store because the removal of unwanted coupling is carried out by programming to destroy the unnecessary connections. (PROM is the registered trade mark of Harris Semiconductors.)

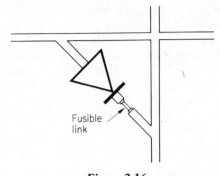

Figure 2.16

Although it has given good results, the fusible link technique has appeared suspect to some people who consider that it has two dangerous characteristics: either the link may re-establish itself; or short-circuits may be caused by particles of metal generated when the fusing occurs. In order to overcome these problems it has been proposed that the coupling connections should not be broken (that is, melted), but should be made highly resistive. In this case the aluminium link is replaced by a nichrome connection and thus a high current, instead of causing it to melt, makes it oxidise. The necessary oxygen is supplied by the surrounding air, or partly given up by silicon oxide.

At present the fusible technique is more common in bipolar read-only memories including modules having a capacity of not more than 512 bits.

2.5.3 Diode or Transistor

In figure 2.15 the coupling between word wire and bit wire is made by a diode. In practice the majority of manufacturers currently prefer to use transistor coupling, since its electrical qualities are much better. Two methods of transistor coupling exist: bipolar TTL and MOS. Broadly speaking the latter yields capacities ten times greater and access times ten times slower than for TTL. However, considerable advances are currently being made on the access times of read-only memories using MOS transistors. For example there are packages of 4096 bits (made up of 512 words of 8 bits) with access times of 150 to 300 ns.

Generally speaking capacities range from 128 to 4096 bits/package, organised in words of 1,2,4 or 8 bits.

It should be noted that when transistor coupling is used, the fusible or oxidisable connection is generally found in the transistor base (or gate for a MOST), though in some designs it is placed in the emitter.

2.6 Modifiable Memories: Ovonic Interrupters

This type of memory belongs to the family of integrated circuits and this shares all the advantages of integrated technology. On the other hand it allows a modification of the memory contents, giving the versatility that is lacking in read-only stores.

The coupling between word and bit wires (figure 2.17) is made by a diode in series with a two-state resistance called an ovonic interrupter, after the physicist Ovshinsky. This resistance is made of a 'glass'-type material which can exist in two physical states, crystalline or amorphous, exhibiting two very different values of electrical resistance, one low and the other high.

In order to obtain the high-resistance amorphous state a sufficient current is passed through the material to heat it and cause it to lose its crystalline state; for example, a current providing $5\,\mu J$ in $5\,\mu s$ for a cylindrical ovonic interrupter of $5\,\mu m$ diameter and $1.5\,\mu m$ thickness. Such a cell cools to the ambient temperature within $1\,\mu s$, the cooling being sufficiently rapid to prevent the device reverting to the crystalline state.

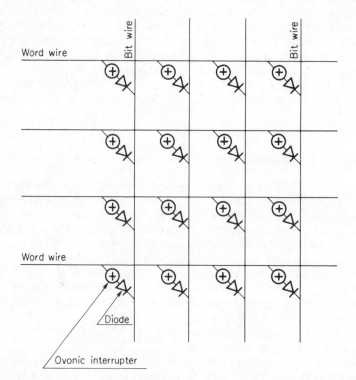

Figure 2.17

To return to the low-resistance crystalline state, another electronic phenomenon is involved, namely the displacement of carriers, which causes an atomic restructuring. Carrier displacement is obtained by applying a voltage in excess of a certain threshold value to the amorphous material.*

Apart from ovonic interrupters, the majority of reprogrammable ROMs (hence the name REPROM) are based on the principle of storing an electric charge on the gate of an insulated gate field-effect transistor. If the gate dielectric is sufficiently good, the stored charge can bias the transistor into a conductive state for a considerable period of time. In practice it is sufficient for this time to be somewhat longer than the lifetime of the computer. However, with the aid of an outside agency (electric pulse, radiation, etc.) the stored charge can at any time be replaced or dissipated in order to rewrite or 'refresh' the contents of a memory.

Such a technique is currently used in the REPROMs called FAMOS (Floating-gate Avalanche-injection MOS) marketed by the INTEL Corporation. The charge on the insulated gate is obtained by an electric pulse of about −30 V, and erasure is obtained simply by submitting the module to ultraviolet radiation.†

*For further information, see 'Amorphous Semiconductors', parts I and II, *Electronics*, September 28, 1970, pp. 56–60 and 61–72.
†For further information, see Dov Frohman-Beutchkowsky, 'A Fully Decoded 2048-bit Electrically Programmable FAMOS Read-Only Memory', in *Semiconductor Memories*, I.E.E.E. Press, 1972, pp. 146–51.

3 The Microinstruction

A microinstruction has four primary functions

(a) the designation of micro-operations to be carried out;

(b) the designation of a subsequent microinstruction; that is, specifying the address of the next microinstruction in the micro-program;

(c) the indication of the duration of the microinstruction either by specifying

(i) the time delay before moving to the next microinstruction, or by providing

(ii) a conditional signal to indicate the completion of the current microinstruction;

(d) the definition of special microprogram functions, such as parity control.

The microinstruction word has four parts which correspond to these four functions. We shall call them micro-operations, next address, delay function, and special bits.

Some of these functions can be implicit and this is usually the case for the next address of the microinstruction of address n; the following one being found at address $n + 1$. For such microinstructions the 'micro-operations' part would be able to occupy more space and be richer as a consequence. Similarly, the delay function will be absent if it has been decided that all microinstructions are to have the same duration and the hardware has been designed accordingly.

3.1 Microinstruction Format

There are three basic methods of designing the microinstruction layout

(a) microinstructions with independent fields coded separately;

(b) instruction-type microinstructions;

(c) microinstructions with independent fields coded globally.

We shall describe the first two methods using existing examples, and differences between them will quickly become apparent. For further clarification we shall treat a particular example using the first two methods; then, having identified the main problems, we will present the third method.

3.1.1 Microinstructions with Independent Fields Coded Separately

A structure using microinstructions with independent fields coded separately is typical of microprogramming; it aims to reflect the real functioning of the computer in the micro-operation itself.

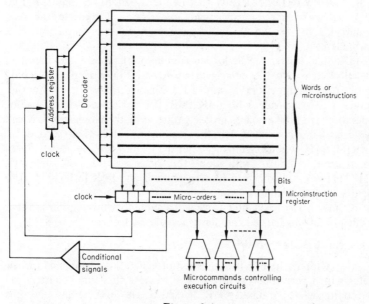

Figure 3.1

As described in chapter 1 the microinstruction is divided into fixed length sub-words called 'fields'. Each field has a corresponding decoding circuit which uses the bits of the field to generate the microcommands (figure 3.1). The fields are independent in the sense that the decoding of each one is, as a rule, independent of the decoding of the others. For example, one field will control the data flow to or from a particular bus while another field will provide commands for the central store.

Example of Microprogram Writing   Let us write the microprogram corresponding to the fetch phase in table 1.1, for the computer shown in chapter 1, figure 1.5. First we will decide upon the format of the microinstruction word, as shown below.

MAR	M	MR	IC	Bus A input	ALU	–	CU status bits

Next we must determine the number of bits and the coding for each field.

MAR: this register must be either loaded or left unchanged and thus a single bit is sufficient for this field. It will be assumed that a 1 commands a loading into MAR.

M: this field controls the main store and therefore it must designate a READ, a WRITE, or signify that neither operation is required. Two bits are sufficient for this field: the first will indicate the read command, the second the write command. (The combination 11 is forbidden.)

MR: this register can be loaded from M or bus B or not be modified at all. Hence two bits are again sufficient. For example, 01 could indicate a loading from M and 10 a loading from bus B. Another solution is to provide a bit mIR [MR] [0] to indicate that a loading operation is to take place. (After gating with the clock signal, it will serve as microcommand for the loading of MR.) The second bit mIR [MR] [1] will determine whether the loading is to be made from M or from bus B. We will adopt the latter solution and use mIR [MR] [1] = 1 to indicate a loading from B and mIR [MR] [1] = 0 to signify loading from M.

IC: in contrast to chapter 1, we will assume that this register is either loaded or left unchanged and hence a single bit suffices

(mIR [IC]) = Load/IC

Bus A input: here it is a question of generating commands for the gates which permit access to bus A. First note that three registers can be connected to A, namely MR, IC and R. However, at any one time only one register can be connected to A and thus two bits are sufficient for this field. For example

(mIR [bus A input] [0,1])	*Action*
00	no register connected
01	MR selected, that is, command OP/MR & A
10	OP/IC & A
11	OP/R & A

ALU: the field controlling the ALU is rather dependent on the ALU itself, and to avoid the detailed coding of this field we will simply enter the name of the ALU operation. For example (+) will be used for +/ALU, (+1) will be used for +1/ALU, etc.

CU status bits: if we refer back to figure 1.11, we see that three situations occur

during a given phase: ADV/C MAR [least-significant bits] at the end of a fetch phase and the start of an execution
RESET/C MAR [least significant] and Load/C MAR [most significant]
at the end of an execution:
RESET/C MAR [least significant] and RESET/C MAR [most significant]

Since a total of 3 situations exists, the coding requires 2 bits; we shall thus adopt the following conventions

01/AVD/C MAR [least significant]
11/RESET/C MAR [least significant] and Load/C MAR [most significant]
10/RESET/C MAR [least significant] and RESET/C MAR [most significant]
00/ no significance

Note that we have not given an example of conditional jump within the microprograms. In practice such a jump can occur quite frequently; however to simplify the present discussion we shall defer the treatment of this problem to later in the chapter.

Taking into account the above conventions (which are summarised in table 3.1) we can write the binary microprogram corresponding to table 1.1 complete with the updating of the CU status bits. This microprogram is stored in the command store as shown below, the symbol $\emptyset$ indicating that it is immaterial whether the control store contains 1 or 0. (A $\emptyset$ would be chosen if, for example, coupling 0 costs less than coupling 1.)

	MAR	M	MR	IC	Bus A input	ALU		CU status bits
Page 0, word 0	1	00	0$\emptyset$	0	10	(+1)	–	01
word 1	0	10	0$\emptyset$	1	1 0	(+)	–	0 1
2	0	10	0$\emptyset$	0	0 0	$\emptyset$	–	0 1
3	0	10	10	0	0 0	$\emptyset$	–	0 1
4	0	01	0$\emptyset$	0	0 1	$\emptyset$	–	0 1
5	0	01	0$\emptyset$	0	0 0	$\emptyset$	–	1 1
6	0	01	0$\emptyset$	0	0 0	$\emptyset$	–	0 1

Table 3.1

MAR	M	MR	IC	Bus A Input	ALU	—	Status bits

MAR	1 bit	1 = load 0 = no load
M	2 bits	00 = do nothing 01 = write 10 = read 11 = illegal
MR	2 bits	00 01 no load 10 = load MR from M 11 = load MR from B
IC	1 bit	1 = load 0 = no load
Bus A input	2 bits	00 = no reg connected 01 = MR selected 10 = IC selected 11 = R selected
ALU		+/ALU +1/ALU
CU status bits		01 ADV C MAR [least sig] 11 RESET C MAR [least sig] and LOAD C MAR [most sig] 10 RESET C MAR [least sig] and RESET C MAR [most sig] 00 No significance

In the same way we can write the two microinstructions of the addition
instruction

Page add, word								
0	0	00	0∅	0	11	+	—	10
word 1	0	00	0∅	0	00	imma- terial	—	01

Note There is a predominance of zeros in the microprogram. This
is in basic agreement with the photograph on page 20 where the
number of diodes is much less than half the number of possible
couplings.

As the operation described by the microprogram becomes more
complex, it is advisable to clarify the problem by drawing a flowchart

before writing the sequence of microinstructions. For example, consider the instruction microprogram

$$(R) \longrightarrow M[M[(IC) + (ACC)]]$$

In this case the problem may be clarified by drawing up the following flowchart

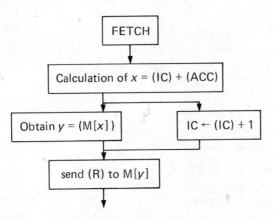

IBM 360-30 Computer This is a good example of a computer having microprogrammed control using a field-structured microinstruction word. IBM engineers have published a large amount of literature on this subject and we have drawn particularly on articles by H. Weber, S. G. Tucker and N. Wirth. (The simplified diagrams of figures 3.1 and 3.2 are similar to those presented by these authors.) In the diagram of figure 3.2 each component is associated with a particular control field: for example CC for the ALU, CB for the bus B, etc. (Note that input and output devices and those relating to the internal control of malfunctions, breakdowns, etc. are not shown.)

The basic cycle of the control memory is 0.75 μs. During each cycle

(1) The information can circulate from each of the 8-bit general registers I, J, ... to another general register via the ALU. The method of operation of registers A and B is therefore technologically rather special.

(2) Register R serves as input/output register for the main store. Information can be transmitted from one of the general registers into the address register of the main store and from an addressed memory location into R. At the same time, the addressed storage location is reset to zero (that is, a destructive read cycle).

(3) An addressed memory location can be loaded with the contents of register R (write cycle).

(4) The microinstruction register is loaded with the contents of the addressed word in the read-only control store. Also the address register

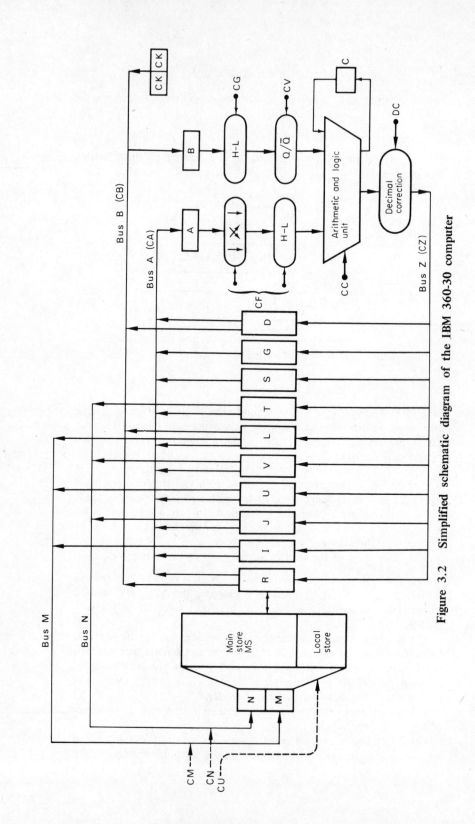

Figure 3.2 Simplified schematic diagram of the IBM 360-30 computer

of the control store is loaded from the next address part of the microinstruction register.

LINK Microcommands Fields CA, CB and CZ determine which registers are connected to buses A, B and Z respectively.

Value of field CA/CZ	Register connected on A/Z
0 0 0 0 to 0 1 0 1	(no register connected)
0 1 1 0	S
0 1 1 1	R
1 0 0 0	D
1 0 0 1	L
1 0 1 0	G
1 0 1 1	T
1 1 0 0	V
1 1 0 1	U
1 1 1 0	J
1 1 1 1	I

Value of field CB	Register connected on B
0 0	R
0 1	L
1 0	D
1 1	CK

CK is part of the output register of the read-only store.
CK comprises 4 bits that are simultaneously directed to the 4 most significant bits and the 4 least significant bits of bus B.

Control of the Main Store Fields CM and CU control the operation of the core store. In effect the memory is partitioned into two areas, the main store and the local store. The latter is a small extension to the main memory and is used as a set of general registers by the CPU. For example these general registers are available for register-to-register operations. (Note that the local store is not directly accessible by the 360 programmer.) Field CU is a single-bit field that determines which of the stores, local or main, is to be involved in the current microinstruction. The second memory control field CM, is used in the following way

Field CM

0 0 0	non-functioning
0 0 1 0 1 0 0 1 1	read cycles. Address supplied (respectively) by the pairs of registers IJ, UV and LT. Information obtained from the memory is placed in register R. Reading has destroyed the content of the addressed store location.
1 0 1 1 1 0 1 1 1	as above, but without the loading of register R.
1 0 0	write. The contents of the location, whose address was supplied when the last read cycle occurred, are loaded into register R.

The CN field is used in a similar way.

Control of Arithmetic and Logic Unit   Fields CF and CG determine the use of the two 4-bit parts (HI for the most-significant 4-bits, LO for the least-significant 4-bits) of the 8-bit registers A and B.

Fields CF

0 0 0	inhibit the transmission of HI and LO	The first bit thus controls the swopping of HI and
0 0 1	inhibit HI and connect LO	LO. The second bit
0 1 0	connect HI and inhibit LO	controls the transmission
0 1 1	connect HI and LO	of HI. The third bit controls

1 0 0 ⎫
1 0 1 ⎪ first HI and LO are
1 1 0 ⎬ interchanged and then   the transmission of LO.
1 1 1 ⎭ the above connections
     are used.

Field CG

0 0	inhibit the transmission of HI and LO
0 1	inhibit HI, connect LO
1 0	connect HI, inhibit LO
1 1	connect HI and LO

Field CV

The transfer of register B to the ALU, either directly or in its bit-complemented form, is controlled by this field.

Field CC

Field CC controls the operation of the ALU itself and is used in the manipulation of carrys.

Value of CC	Operation
0 0 0	Addition. Carry In = 0
0 0 0	Carry In = 1
0 1 0	AND
0 1 1	OR
1 0 0	Addition. Carry In = 0 ⎫
1 0 1	Addition. Carry In = 1 ⎬ Carry Out stored in C
1 1 0	Addition. Carry In = C ⎭
1 1 1	Exclusive OR

The above description of the IBM 369-30 demonstrates the field structure of this computer and provides some detail regarding the individual field coding. Later we shall see the use of some of the other fields. In particular, addressing will be covered in section 3.4.

3.1.2 Microinstruction with 'Instruction Type' Structure

Microprogramming using this format has been inspired by the elementary machine languages of the late 1950s. Here, operands and an operation code can be defined. The operation code fixes the significance of the remainder of the microinstruction and defines the principal operation to be performed. This format describes the result of the microinstruction rather than the operands necessary to produce the result, and machines using this technique usually have short but powerful microinstructions. This technique is useful when a non-specialist is to microprogram a computer.

The term mini-instruction is also used to describe this type of microinstruction; one then speaks of *miniprogramming*. This comes close to the concept put forward by Wilkes: that an instruction is executed by a sequence of information transfers from register to register. Hence the idea of creating a set of mini-instructions which describe these information transfers. Mini-instructions only refer to registers and, since these are small in number, the words are short.

Microprogramming of this type is often adopted for small computers since it leads to short words of, for example, 16 bits. These short words can even be put into the central core store, though it is usual to use a reserved area of core which is inaccessible to the normal programmer.

It is therefore desirable for the central store to be organised in words of such a length as to make it easy to store the microprogram. The simplest approach is for program words (data or instructions) and microprogram words to be of the same length. In adopting this strategy a designer retains the possibility of modifying the computer by using a faster microprogram memory technology, and has the facility for using both a fast but permanent read-only store and the less rapid but writable central memory.

As an example of a computer based on this type of microinstruction we shall examine the Multi-8 computer, manufactured in France by Intertechnique.

Multi-8 Computer   Figure 3.3 shows a simplified diagram of the Multi-8. The basic cycle lasts 220 ns and all 16 microinstructions available on the Multi-8 are interpreted according to the following format (designation of the next microinstruction is not included).

15	12 11	0
Operation code	Control	

The 4 bits of the operation code define the micro-operation(s) to be carried out. Bits 11 to 0 usually define the different parameters necessary for the execution of the microinstruction, though for certain types of microinstruction this part can be interpreted as a constant.

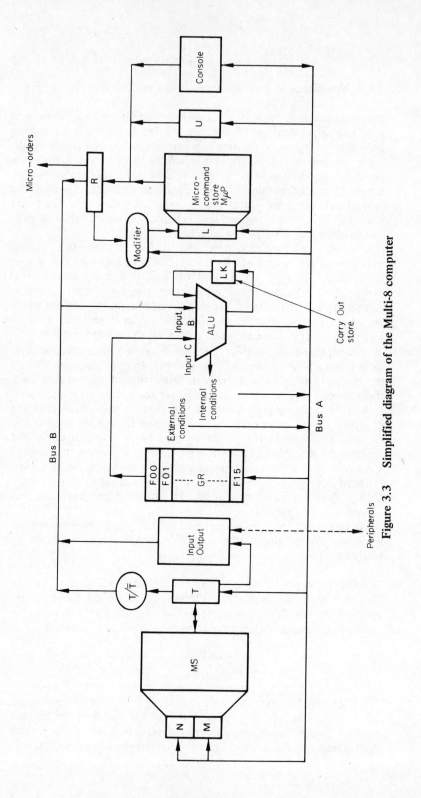

Figure 3.3   Simplified diagram of the Multi-8 computer

Each microinstruction requires 1 or 2 cycles for its execution, or in other words 220 or 440 ns.

Classification of Microinstructions   The microinstructions available on the Multi-8 are grouped into three distinct categories; these are operational microinstructions, associated constant microinstructions, and special microinstructions. For each category we shall briefly describe the role of control bits and give some examples of the microinstructions.

The following conventions will be adopted

(a) The 16 general registers are denoted F00, F01, F02, ... F15.

(b) The register F00 is the condition register; it stores both internal arithmetic conditions and the external conditions.

(c) LK designates the memory element storing the carry output from the ALU.

Operational Microinstructions Microinstructions in this category control register-to-register transfers, as well as the manipulation of data inside the processing unit, the core store and the input/output system. The general format of these microinstructions is

15	12	11	8	7	4	3	0
Operation code		General address register		Control bits		Destination	

Bits 11 to 8 designate one of the 16 general registers, whose contents will serve as an operand. Bits 7 to 4 control the operation. Generally bit 7 indicates if (LK) serves as input carry. However, if this bit is zero, bit 6 gives the value of the input carry. Bit 5 determines whether (T) is to be used as an operand.

If bit 3 = 0 the general register specified by bits 11 to 8 is to be used both as the source and destination of information flow during the microinstruction. Conversely if bit 3 = 1 the specified general register is not used as a destination.

The three bits 2 to 0 define a second destination register according to the table shown below.

Bits 2 1 0	Destination D
0 0 0	No destination is specified
0 0 1	T
0 1 0	M
0 1 1	N
1 0 0	L (with $0 \rightarrow$ L [8])
1 0 1	L (with $1 \rightarrow$ L [8])
1 1 0	U
1 1 1	U V $(M\mu P) \rightarrow$ R

Some examples of operational microinstructions are

Addition and incrementation
   Code: 8 (1000 in binary form)
   (execution time: 1 cycle)
   Condition register: unchanged if bit $4 = 0$, modified if bit $4 = 1$
Description

$$(F) + (T) + 1 + (LK) \longrightarrow D$$
$$\llcorner \blacktriangleright \text{If bit } 7 = 1$$
$$\llcorner \blacktriangleright \text{If bit } 6 = 1$$
$$\llcorner \blacktriangleright \text{If bit } 5 = 1$$

If carry then $1 \longrightarrow LK$
If no carry then $0 \longrightarrow LK$

The content of the register F is added to the content of register T. The result is transferred to the destination register(s) specified by D.

The state of the link bit LK, before addition, is added to the sum if bit $7 = 1$.

The sum is incremented by 1 if bit $6 = 1$. Furthermore, LK is reset to zero if there is no carry, and loaded with 1 if a carry exists.

Subtraction
   Code: 9 (1001)
   Execution time: 1 cycle
   Condition register: may be modified if bit $4 = 1$ (depending on the result of the operation), and is unchanged if bit $4 = 0$.
Description

$$(F) + (\bar{T}) + (T) + 1 + (LK) \longrightarrow D$$
$$\llcorner \blacktriangleright \text{If bit } 7 = 1$$
$$\llcorner \blacktriangleright \text{If bit } 6 = 0 \text{ and bit } 7 = 0$$
$$\llcorner \blacktriangleright \text{If bit } 5 = 0$$

If carry then 1 $\longrightarrow LK$
If no carry then $0 \longrightarrow LK$

The contents of register F are added to the complemented contents of register T to provide the operation of subtraction. The result is placed in destination D.

The uncomplemented contents of register T can be included in the sum (along with F) depending on the state of bit 5. This rather unusual operation provides an example of the 'gymnastics' that are possible with a microprogrammed machine.

Shifts
    Code: 15 (1111)
    Execution time: 1 cycle
    Condition register: unchanged if bit 4 = 0, modified depending on the result of the operation, if bit 4 = 1.
    Bit 5 determines the direction of the shift
    (i)   If bit 5 = 0, then $(F[1,7]) \rightarrow D[0,6]$
            if bit 6 = 1, then $1 \rightarrow D[7]$
            if bit 7 = 1, then $(LK) \rightarrow D[7]$ and $(F[0]) \rightarrow LK$
    (ii)   if bit 5 = 1, then $(F[0,6]) \rightarrow D[1,7]$
            if bit 6 = 1, then $1 \rightarrow D[0]$
            if bit 7 = 1, then $[LK) \rightarrow D[0]$ and $(F[7]) \rightarrow LK$

Associated Constant Microinstructions   Classified in this group are the microinstructions controlling the manipulation of constants from the microprogram store. The general format is

15	12	11	8	7	0
Operation code		General address register F		Constant C	

We shall give two examples of such microinstructions

Loading a constant into a general register
    Code: 2 (0010)
    Execution time: 1 cycle
    Condition register: unchanged
Description

$$C \longrightarrow F$$

Comparison
    Code: 6 (0110)
    Execution time: if 'less than': 1 cycle

        if 'greater than or equal to': 2 cycles

    Condition register: unchanged
Description
        Result $= (F) + C$
        If result $< 2^8$, $(L) + 1 \longrightarrow L$
        If result $\geqslant 2^8$, $(L) + 2 \longrightarrow L$
    An arithmetic sum is carried out between the content of the general register F and the constant C. If this sum is greater than or equal to 2^8 (an overflow) the next microinstruction is skipped. Alternatively if an overflow does not occur $(<2^8)$ the next

microinstruction is executed in sequence. Register F remains unchanged during this operation.

Special microinstructions   We shall give three examples

To execute
Code: 0 (0000)
Execution time: 1 cycle for an 'ineffective' code (non-operation)
For other codes see execution time of the corresponding microinstruction
Description

$$(M\mu P[15,8]) \vee (U[7,0]) \longrightarrow R[15,8)$$

followed by the execution of the microinstruction contained in R.

(U is an 8-bit register)

The 'execute' microinstruction is taken from the micro-program store MμP and modified by the contents of the register U before being obeyed. If the content of register U is itself equal to zero, a non-operation function (NOP) will be executed.
In the case where the resultant microinstruction modifies register U, it is the content of this register before execution that is used to construct the microinstruction.

Loading of a constant into M

$$(R[0,6]) \longrightarrow M$$

The constant held in bits 0 to 6 of the microinstruction is loaded into the most significant 7 bits of register M, thus allowing the selection of a 256-word page in the memory.

External interrupt enable (EINT)
This microinstruction allows external interrupts to be serviced. When the 'external interrupt' line is in the logical 1 state, it is transferred directly into bit 7 of the condition register, provided the interrupts have been enabled by EINT. If the interrupts are not enabled the interrupt line is ignored.

3.1.3 A Comparison of 'Field' and 'Instruction' Forms of Microinstruction

Let us consider the circuit of figure 3.4. In a field structure, there will be

(a) a field CV to indicate that the operand B is transmitted directly or bit-complemented. (1 bit)

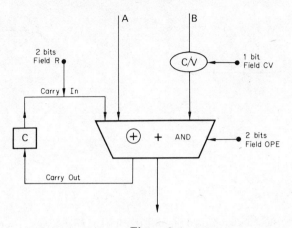

Figure 3.4

(b) a field OPE to specify the functioning of the operator (that is, operations +, $\oplus$ or AND). (2 bits)

(c) a field R of 2 bits indicating the 'Carry In' used during the arithmetical addition operation

    (i)   Carry In equal to zero

    (ii) Carry In equal to 1

    (iii) Carry In equal to the previous Carry Out, that is, the state stored in bistable C.

The field-structured approach therefore requires a total of 5 bits.

If however it is accepted that bit-complementation is only used either in isolation or at the same time as addition, then the necessary operations may be broken down into the following form

$\bar{B}$	$A + B + C$
$A + B$	$A + \bar{B} + C$
$\bar{B} + 1$	$A \oplus B$
$A + \bar{B} + 1$	A AND B

If the 8 operations are coded using 3 bits, a 2-bit saving may be achieved, albeit at the cost of a more complex decoding network and a limitation in the number of possibilities for extending the operation codes.

3.1.4 The Concept of a Controlled Graph

A graph is a natural figure to draw in order to symbolise a set of entities, some of which are linked by a relationship. These entities are represented by points (called vertices) and the linking relationships are shown as lines joining the vertices (called edges). If A is linked to B, an edge incorporating an arrow is drawn from A towards B; however, it

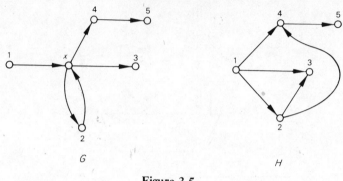

Figure 3.5

should be noted that this does not imply that there is an arrow from B towards A. Figure 3.5 shows some examples.

If there is a reverse direction for every arrow, then the graph is said to be symmetrical. This in turn allows us to define a non-symmetrical or directed graph.

Connectivity Matrix of a Graph   This is a square binary matrix possessing a row and column for each vertex. If vertex i is linked to vertex j, the matrix has a 1 at the intersection of row i and column j. Alternatively if no connection exists the matrix element takes the value 0.

The connectivity matrices associated with the graphs G and H (figure 3.5) are respectively

	G								H				
	1	2	3	4	5	x			1	2	3	4	5
1	0	0	0	0	0	1		1	0	1	1	1	0
2	0	0	0	0	0	1		2	0	0	1	1	0
3	0	0	0	0	0	0		3	0	0	0	0	0
4	0	0	0	0	1	0		4	0	0	0	0	1
5	0	0	0	0	1	0		5	0	0	0	0	1
x	0	1	1	1	0	0							

Instruction   We shall define an instruction as a function or mapping P, of the set of edges of graph G onto a new graph G_p, where G_p is a partial graph of G.

An alternative way of viewing this mapping is to point out that the connectivity matrix M_p of the partial graph G_p is a partial matrix of the connectivity matrix M of graph G. Hence M_p is a matrix obtained by suppressing some of the 1s in the matrix M and by replacing them by 0s.

In the following discussion we shall simply define an instruction as a partial matrix P of the matrix M. For example, for the graph G given above, two partial graphs, that is instructions (and the corresponding partial matrices) are shown below

$$1 \longrightarrow x \longrightarrow 3 \qquad\qquad 2 \longrightarrow x \longrightarrow 4$$

0		0		0			0		0		0

0	0	0	0	0	1		0	0	0	0	0	0
0	0	0	0	0	0		0	0	0	0	0	1
0	0	0	0	0	0		0	0	0	0	0	0
0	0	0	0	0	0		0	0	0	0	0	0
0	0	0	0	0	0		0	0	0	0	0	0
0	0	1	0	0	0		0	0	0	1	0	0

Controlled Graph   A directed graph G, for which a non-empty set of instructions is defined, is called a controlled graph.

Physical Significance of an Instruction   A term $(i,j) = 1$ of an instruction indicates that a direct path of i towards j is allowed. If $(i,j) = 0$, either there is no direct path of i towards j, or this path, if it exists, is forbidden in the instruction.

A network provided with instructions could take the form of streets controlled by red and green lights, or alternatively a network of operators and electronic memory elements whose connections are controlled by AND gates, as found in a stored program computer.

The Computer as a Controlled Graph   As suggested above the complex interconnection of elements which form a computer can be considered as a network or graph. This graph is a controlled graph if one considers an instruction to be a set of commands for opening AND gates or clocking registers in order to establish the patterns of information flow within the computer. For the moment we will leave aside the question of operator commands (add, subtract, shift, etc.) and focus our attention on the problem of defining interconnections.

In a graph corresponding to a stored-program computer, there is a difference between a vertex representing a purely combinational unit and that representing a sequential device such as a register or counter. A combinational circuit is traversed by the information during an instruction, whereas a sequential unit is more complex in that it involves time-registration of the information. One means of representing the sequential circuit x is to use two vertices x_1 and x_2.

During a particular instruction T, the two nodes are disconnected, so making all terms of the form (x_1, x_2) take the value zero. However, between adjacent instructions in the program sequence, information must flow between vertices x_1 and x_2. In the graph-theory model this is achieved using the implicit instruction denoted by $ for which all terms of

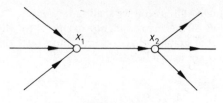

Figure 3.6

the type (x_1, x_2) are equal to 1, while all other terms are zero. This technique does not appear particularly artificial when one considers that for most modern logic technologies, bistables and registers are built using a corresponding master—slave technique.

Note The entity that we have termed an 'instruction' in the context of controlled graphs, corresponds to the concept of 'micro-instruction' in the context of the stored program computer.

3.1.5 Choice of Micro-operation Fields

It should be remembered that two types of command (or rather microcommand) need to be generated: function or operator commands; and connection or link commands.

Function or Operator Commands These commands specify the functioning of certain modules or operators. For example, the arithmetic and logic operator can perform addition, intersection, or union; the main core memory (or strictly the selected word in this memory) can be read, written into, reset to zero or left completely unchanged.

As a rule, a field is adopted for each module identified in this way and when listing all functions for each module, the dormant condition must not be forgotten.

Connection or Link Commands These commands form the controlling inputs to the AND gates of the execution network. In fact, as we have already noted, in some cases AND gate commands are replaced by register loading commands; however, the principle of information transfer remains unchanged. We shall now represent a computer in the form of a graph, restricting ourselves to the links to be controlled.

Figure 3.7 shows the graph for the computer whose block diagram was given in figure 3.3. The problem is to designate certain routes in this graph, or in other words to specify a sub-set of edges that allows the required pattern of information flow. We need to bear in mind the following points.

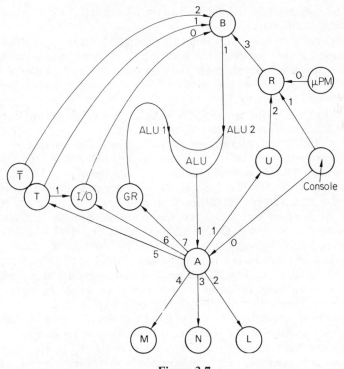

Figure 3.7

(a) There is at most only one source of information connected at a time to a bus or to an operator input.

(b) It is however permissible for a bus to direct its information to several receiving registers. Despite this, it is possible that for logical or electrical reasons, only a single receiver at a time will be admissible. This simplifying assumption will be made below.

(c) Each input of an operator with *n* operands constitutes a vertex. Such is the case with an ALU, whose two inputs will be called ALU1 and ALU2.

Disconnecting Set   In order to designate the information transmitting edges, it is convenient to choose a sufficient set of vertices such that in stating which edges arrive at and leave each vertex in the set we have uniquely described the required information flow. For each edge of the graph being described, at least one of its two vertices must belong to the chosen set. In other words, the vertices are chosen such that, if both they and the edges terminating at them or leaving them are suppressed, the resultant graph will consist only of isolated vertices. Vertices chosen in this way are said to be 'disconnecting' and a set of such vertices is called a disconnecting set.

We should note at this stage that certain vertices require special treatment. These vertices are those at which only one edge arrives and leaves. In these cases we break the edge terminating at a vertex when the operation under consideration does not use the information transmitted by the edge.

In figure 3.7, the sets {A,B,R,ALU,I/O,}, {A,T,R,ALU,I/O} and {A,B,T,R,ALU} are disconnecting sets.

For each disconnecting vertex the presence or absence of an authorised edge must be indicated among the input and output edges. These two indications constitute the input and the output field of this vertex. However, an edge has only to be designated once and, if two disconnecting vertices are adjacent, it is sufficient to count the link edge either as leaving one or entering the other. This can facilitate a closer approach to the ideal solution in which the number of edges entering and leaving each disconnecting vertex is equal to $2^n - 1$; n bits then suffice to indicate along which of the $2^n - 1$ edges the information is passing. (Here the 2^nth combination is reserved for the situation where no information arrives at or leaves the vertex in question.) The number of edges arriving on a bus (or at the input of a combinatory operator) can even reach 2^n, provided it can be shown that the information (or the operator result) is not transmitted to another vertex.

As an example, let us consider the disconnecting set {A,B,R,ALU,I/O} (figure 3.7). The following table shows the input and output edges for each element.

Elements		Input edges	Output edges
A		2	7
B		4	1
R		3	1
ALU	input 1	1	output : 1
	input 2	1	
I/O		2	1

However using the property that a given edge need only be designated once, we can reduce the number of edges.

For vertex R the number of outputs is reduced from 1 to 0 because the corresponding edge is already counted as an input for B. This in turn leads to a favourable situation at B which now has 4 input edges and only one output. Thus 2 bits suffice to define one of the 4 input edges and a single bit can be used to control transmission or inhibition of the output edge.

Elements		Input edges	Output edges
A		2	7
B		4	1
R		3	0
ALU	input 1	1	0
	input 2	0	
I/O		1	0

For input 2 of the ALU the input edge is already counted as the output of B, and the output of the ALU is taken as the input of A. For A too there is a favourable coding situation since the 2 input edges can be represented with a single bit and, using a further 3 bits, we can specify one of the 7 output edges as well as the case where A does not transmit the information it receives.

For the I/O element the number of input edges is reduced by one since one of these edges is already counted as an output from A. In addition, the output edge is already accounted for as an input for B.

Finally, we emerge with the following format.

Field	Number of bits
A, input field	1
A, output field	3
B, input field	2
B, output field	1
R, input field	2
Input field on the input 1 of the ALU	1
I/O, input field	1
Total	11

In order to code these fields we shall use the edge numbering of figure 3.7, and ensure that, for each edge, the binary representation of the edge number is the code designating that edge. Hence a micro-instruction such as

$\bar{T} \longrightarrow B$; $B \longrightarrow ALU2$; $GR \longrightarrow ALU1$;
$ALU \longrightarrow A$; $A \longrightarrow U$; $T \longrightarrow I/O$

is written as

1	0 0 1	1 0	1	0 0	1	1
input	output	input	output	R	ALU 1	I/O
A		B				

and a microinstruction

U→R; R→B; B→ALU 2; ALU→A; A→T

takes the form

1	1 0 1	1 1	1	1 0	0	0
input	output	input	output	R	ALU 1	I/O
A		B				

General note   For certain commands, it can be difficult to decide which type (operator or link command) is involved. An example of this occurs in the Multi-8 computer and can be illustrated using figures 3.3 and 3.7. For the output command of the register T towards bus B one can imagine an operator being commanded to yield T or T. Alternatively it might be considered that the register T possesses two outputs T and T̄ and that a choice is made using link commands to connect the appropriate output to the bus. In practice the confusion between these two concepts does not present any particular difficulty.

Figure 3.8 shows the graph of the IBM 360-30 and it is left to the reader to verify that the disconnecting set {A,B,Z,M,N} corresponds closely to the fields described a few pages earlier.

3.1.6 Coding Using Globally Coded Fields

For simplicity we shall again exclude the control of operators and limit our attention to the link type of command. Using this configuration we shall consider the connectivity matrix of the resulting controlled graph of the execution network. Subsequently we shall reduce this matrix by removing certain redundancies. For example a 1 on the matrix corresponding to a permanent (uncontrolled) connection implies that either a row or column may be deleted. Also rows or columns which contain only zeros may be removed. Thus, certain vertices only appear in rows (output of an arithmetic and logic operator), while others only appear in columns (operand inputs for this same operator). This is a logical arrangement since we would not expect the output of an ALU to receive information and similarly it would be inconsistent for an input to such a unit to generate signals. Also for a register T, it will be seen that there is one input (therefore one column) but two outputs, T and T̄, (and hence two rows). These three examples are all found in the matrix on page 58, associated with the controlled graph of the Multi-8 computer. (For the moment we shall not consider the groupings of 1s as shown; also, we shall assume that every blank space is a 0.)

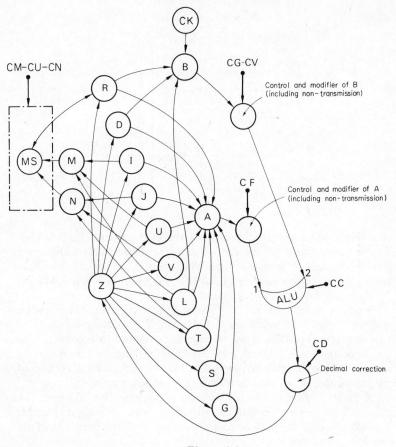

Figure 3.8

Although designing a microinstruction amounts to designating a sub-matrix of the matrix *M*, it should be remembered that all sub-matrices do not constitute valid microinstructions. For example, as already mentioned, only one source of information is connected to a bus at a time. If we also assume that the machine is restricted to having a single information receiver, the sub-matrices of *M* that correspond to valid microinstructions are those with at most a single 1 per row or column.

Designating a microinstruction therefore reduces either to describing the corresponding sub-matrix of *M*, or simply designating this sub-matrix by its number in the finite-size list of valid sub-matrices.

The first method is adopted when the microinstruction fields are coded separately. In effect choosing a disconnecting set amounts to

Multi-8 matrix (modified)

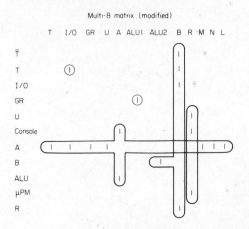

choosing a set of vertices whose rows and columns are such that each non-zero element of the matrix M belongs to this set. This is illustrated for the matrix associated with the Multi-8, in which we have emphasised the disconnecting sets {A,B,R,T,GR} or {A,B,R,I/O,ALU 1} by encircling the appropriate elements.

It will be noted that these connectivity matrices include very few 1s, and the method of independent fields coded separately, amounts to superimposing a sufficient set of rows and columns to account for all the 1s on the matrix. Hence a microinstruction and the corresponding sub-matrix may be specified by indicating, for each row and column of the superimposed set, the position of the non-zero element.

If in the example of the Multi-8, we assume that at most one information receiver is connected to a bus, the eight possible configurations of the sub-row corresponding to the output field of the bus A, can be described with 3 bits

Value of the matrix row corresponding to A	Description
0000000	null row: no receiver is connected to the bus A
1000000	the receiver register T is connected to the bus
0100000	the receiver register I/O is connected to the bus
0010000	the receiver register GR* is connected to the bus
0001000	the receiver register U is connected to the bus A
0000100	the receiver register M is connected to the bus A
0000010	the receiver register N is connected to the bus A
0000001	the receiver register L is connected to the bus A

*It is assumed that the choice between the 16 general registers, GR, is made elsewhere.

The second, more global method suggested above for specifying microinstructions involved enumerating all possible microinstructions in a list, and then designating the required microinstruction with a binary number representing its position in the list. First, the set of micro-instructions must be numbered. For this purpose we define on the matrix M a set of rows and columns corresponding to a disconnecting set. Now we form a 'cross' using the row and the column associated with each element of the chosen disconnecting set.

A convenient method of calculating the size of the set of sub-matrices is to determine the number of possible 'sub-crosses' for each disconnecting element and to compute the product of the numbers thus obtained. However, in this calculation a 1 common to two crosses must be counted only once. As a consequence, certain crosses can be reduced to one row or one column, or even a single square, the latter being the case for $(T, I/O)$ in the Multi-8 matrix.

For a bus, the set of possible sub-crosses is $p \times q + 1$, where p is the number of 1s of the column, and q = the number of 1s of the row. This can be seen by using the single source and a single information receiver assumption, and noting that the bus either links one of the possible p inputs to one of the possible q outputs, or provides no linkage at all.

For a register the situation is slightly different and the number of possible sub-crosses is given by $(p + 1) \cdot (q + 1)$. In this case the input may be obtained by forming one of the possible p links, or alternatively the input might be completely disconnected. Similarly the register output could take one of the $p + 1$ possible configurations.

Allowing for the fact that 1s belonging to two crosses are only counted once, it is possible to have $p = 0$ or $q = 0$.

For the crosses given on the Multi-8 matrix, the result is as follows

$$\text{bus A} \longrightarrow 7 \times 2 + 1 = 15$$

$$\text{bus B} \longrightarrow 4 \times 1 + 1 = 5$$

$$\text{register R} \longrightarrow (0 + 1) \cdot (3 + 1) = 4$$

$$\text{register T} \longrightarrow (1 + 1) \cdot (0 + 1) = 2$$

$$\text{register GR} \longrightarrow (1 + 1) \cdot (0 + 1) = 2$$

This gives a total of $2 \times 2 \times 4 \times 5 \times 15 = 1200$ microinstructions which would be represented by a binary number of 11 bits.

It should be pointed out that in some cases the above total may be inaccurate, since a sub-matrix can be counted twice. Nevertheless the result, if it is in error, is generally only slightly greater than the number of possible microinstructions. Taking the general case we will assume that N microinstructions are coded using n bits such that $2^{n-1} < N \leqslant 2^n$. Then, taking $B = \{0,1\}$ and using the notation B^n to represent the set of binary codes in the range 0 to $2^n - 1$, a specific microinstruction is allocated an n-bit binary number using a one-to-one mapping h

$$\{\mu_i\} \xrightarrow{\ h\ } B^n$$

where $\{\mu_i\}$ is the set of microinstructions.

The mapping simultaneously attaches a *boolean function* (of n variables) to each bit of matrix M, and therefore to each link command. If b is a bit of M, the boolean function associated with b is that whose representatives of the set B^n are given by

$$\left\{\mu_i \mid b = 1 \text{ in } \mu_i\right\} \xrightarrow{\ h\ } \left\{\text{Subset of } B^n \text{ for which } b = 1\right\}$$

Application of Global Coding of Independent Fields to the IBM 360-30 Structure Consider the matrix M associated with the controlled graph (figure 3.8) of the IBM 360-30 (see figure 3.2). If we bear in mind that

(a) for buses A and B the case of non-transmission is already considered in other fields of the microinstruction (fields CF and CG),

(b) the pairs of registers I and J, U and V, and L and T are connected via buses B and M—N, and each forms a single register of 16 bits;

then the list of microinstructions is established as follows

$$\text{bus Z} \longrightarrow 10 + 1 = 11$$
$$\text{bus A} \longrightarrow 10$$
$$\text{bus B} \longrightarrow 4$$
$$\text{bus M—N} \longrightarrow 3 + 1 = 4$$

giving $11 \times 10 \times 4 \times 4 = 110 \times 2^4$ microinstructions, a total that is codable with 11 bits. Hence if we apply global field coding to the 360-30 structure 11 bits are needed for bus control; a number which represents a reduction on the corresponding 14 bits used in the actual 360-30 design.

Note in passing that the field M—N is already globally coded since it represents the address field of the main memory.

Global Coding Applied to Operator Commands The principles governing the global coding of linking operations can also be applied to operator command. Again a product is formed, but in this case the terms of the product represent the number of possible commands for each operator. (Note that the situation where an operator is unused must be included in the count of possible commands for that operator.) As with link commands, the set of possible operator commands is mapped (coded) onto the set of binary numbers containing the appropriate number of bits.

Connection matrix for the 360-30
(blanks are equivalent to nil cases)

	R	I	J	U	V	L	T	S	G	D	A	B	M–N
R											1	1	
I											1		1
J											1		1
U											1		1
V											1		1
L											1	1	1
T											1		1
S											1		
G											1		
D											1	1	
CK												1	
Z	1	1	1	1	1	1	1	1	1	1			

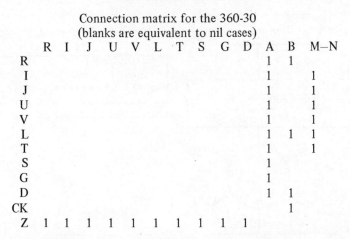

Global Coding Involving Both Operator and Link Commands   In this case the total number of commands is given by the product number of link commands and the number of operator commands.

   Note   If a bus or an operator participates in the total number of commands by a factor of the form 2^i, there is little point in combining it in the total since it can be coded, without any redundancy, using the i bits $X_1, X_2, \ldots X_i$. Alternatively during the synthesis of the command functions, it is important to identify the fact that the 2^i commands of the given operator or bus depend only on the i bits $X_1, X_2, \ldots X_i$.

Conclusions Regarding Global Coding   The main problems associated with global coding are those concerning the difficulties of coding and decoding and any time penalties that these processes may incur. However, even if the separate coding of fields is adopted in a somewhat *a priori* manner, it is still useful to calculate the comparative ROM saving obtained using a global coding technique.

3.2 Organisation of a Set of Microprograms

In operation, a computer continually follows the basic fetch/execute cycle

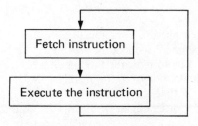

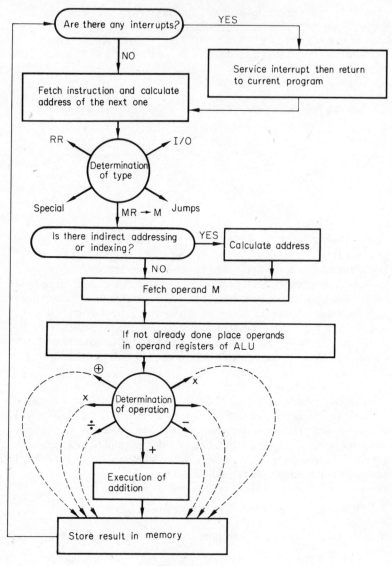

Figure 3.9

Since the fetch phase is common to all instructions the corresponding microprogrammed sequences need only be written once. This
example prompts us to look for those sequences which are common to
several instructions; moreover the machine designer will try to define
the instructions so that they can be grouped into types that are treated
in a similar way. For example, within the set consisting of a particular

type of instruction, the fetching of operands and the storing of the results might well follow a constant format and could therefore be treated as a common sequence.

The microprogram corresponding to an instruction may be broken down into a 'common denominator' string of sequences into which is inserted a specific, and usually quite short, sequence for the particular instruction.

It is desirable for the operation codes to reflect the classification of the instruction types. In this way the microprogramming can be usefully simplified; for example specific parts of the operation code are generally used to determine the microprogram starting address for the relevant instruction classification.

The overlapping of the common areas of different microprograms is illustrated in figure 3.9. This diagram shows the common framework for instructions with two operands (one in register R, the other in central memory M) and a result which is replaced in the memory.

The decision processes of the shared microprogram format are shown in figure 3.10.

In practice, the structure of this flowchart is rather more complicated. It is desirable to read the operands and begin the operations specified by the instruction as early as possible, for example during decoding. On the other hand, if two or more instructions have an almost identical microprogram flow the aim is to maximise the common sequences and defer the decoding branches as long as possible.

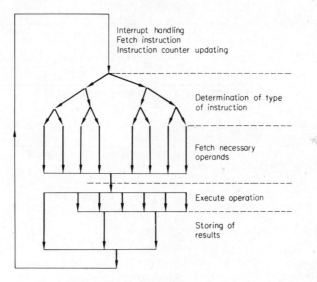

Figure 3.10

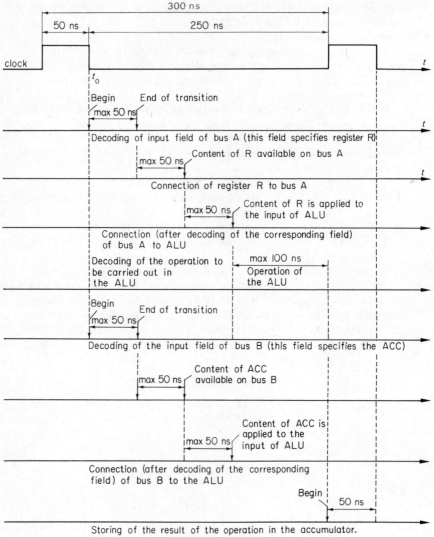

Figure 3.11

Although an organisation of this sort leads to a compact set of microprograms, it has the disadvantage of complicating the choice of the next address in the microinstruction sequence. Furthermore, since these branches are frequently the result of conditional tests, clock cycles may be lost during the branching (see chapter 1, section 1.10). This unfortunate effect can often be avoided, although it usually involves a more complicated calculation of the address of the next microinstruction.

3.3 Timing Diagram of a Read-only Memory Cycle

Using examples taken from the computer shown in figure 1.5, we shall examine some of the detailed operations that occur during a single microinstruction cycle. Although there are technological variations from one computer to another, we shall consider the following fairly typical parameters

(a) the clock pulse H has a width of 50 ns and a period of 300 ns;

(b) only the registers are synchronised; they record the information present on their input when H goes to 1;

(c) the combinational circuits continually use the register output variables. As a result, the functions generated may move through transitory values before stabilising and a suitable delay must occur to allow the circuits to 'settle' before clocking the resultant information into a register. These considerations apply whenever a register takes its input from a combinational circuit and they are equally valid for the input circuits to the microinstruction register.

As an example consider the following instruction (see figure 3.11)

$$(ACC) + (R) \longrightarrow ACC$$

For simplicity, we have assumed that the various small combinational networks have a maximum transmission time of 50 ns, a time extended to 100 ns for the more complex ALU. The result of the operation is not available until time $t_0 + 250$ ns, when it is recorded in the accumulator.

It should be noted that for certain operations, for example, decoding the field specifying the ALU operation, the timing is not critical: slower decoding is therefore acceptable, and this could well allow a more global coding policy to be adopted for this field, or alternatively the required operation could be implemented using slower (and therefore cheaper) logic circuits.

3.4. Next Address Function

We indicated in sections 1.8 and 1.10 the justifications for this function and the problems that it poses. In particular it was found that the principal source of difficulty was the need to introduce considerable overlap (or nesting) in the microprogram sequences in order to reduce their total size. As a consequence, the branches between sequences are multiplied, with the accompanying risks of increased execution time.

When designing a microprogram the aim is to avoid situations where a test for branching towards one address rather than another constitutes a chronological step. In practice the microinstruction specifies the next address as a function of the current address, the operation code and the current state of certain conditional bistables. For example, use could be made of the state (positive, negative or zero) of the result obtained in the course of the present or preceding cycles. Alternatively an overflow or interrupt might provide the conditional information. Generally, it is arranged that the addresses from which a choice is to be made differ only by a few bits so that the next address calculations are restricted in the number of bits they need consider.

For example, we shall call Y the least-significant bit of the address register of the microprogram memory. Then there can be a field of the microinstruction word which, instead of specifying the value of Y, indicates how Y is calculated. A 3-bit field would produce 8 possible microcodes and we shall assume that 000 and 001 are used to force Y to the values 0 or 1. The 6 remaining microcodes can indicate 6 different methods of calculating Y. For example (see the diagram of the 360-30), a microcode could 'put Y to 1 if a carry has been generated by the adder: otherwise Y is put to 0'. This allows a two way microprogram branch depending on the output state of the arithmetic unit.

As a further example, consider the microcode 'put Y to 1 if and only if the least-significant 4 bits of register T are all zero'; this would be useful in the normalisation of a hexadecimal number in register T. Another type of condition often tested is 'put Y to 1 if and only if the leftmost bits of registers T and A are the same', thus allowing a 'branching on the same sign' in the case where this bit is indicative of sign.

What has been said of bit Y can also be applied to other bits, thus allowing, by combining the branching possibilities, switches to 4, 8, . . . routes in the microprograms. We shall give below a typical example of these methods by studying addressing in the read-only memory of the IBM 360-30.

3.4.1 Microprogram Addressing of the IBM 360-30

The address register of the command memory comprises 13 bits, as shown in figure 3.12.

Three parts can be distinguished in the address, each of these being the object of particular treatment as specified by the fields of the

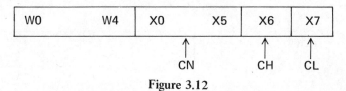

Figure 3.12

microinstruction in operation. Thus, field CL controls X7, field CH controls X6, etc.

From one microinstruction to the next, the 5 most significant bits (W) remain the same unless they are changed by special command generated by a field that we shall not consider in detail (called the 'change of mode' field). In the case in which the W bits are modified, the whole address is changed in an unconditional fashion.

The next six bits X0, ... X5 are specified as a constant by the CN field of the microinstruction.

The remaining two bits X6 and X7 are set according to the conditions specified by the two 4-bit fields CH and CL.

The procedure for setting up the contents of the command memory address register is quite straightforward. There is neither addition, nor incrementation as the quantities (W), (X[0,5]) and (X[6,7]) are simply concatenated as shown in figure 3.13.

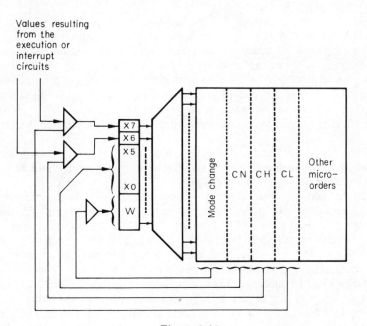

Figure 3.13

CH CL	X6	X7
0 0 0 0	0	0
0 0 0 1	1	1
0 0 1 0	$(R[0])$*	$(R[1])$
0 0 1 1		
0 1 0 0	$(V[6]) \cdot (V[7])$	$(G[1])$
0 1 0 1		$((R[0,3]) \leqslant 9) \cdot ((R[4,7]) \leqslant 9)$
0 1 1 0	$(C[0])$†	$(C[1])$‡
0 1 1 1	$(S[0])$	$((Z[0] \dots Z[7]) = 0)$
1 0 0 0	$(R[2])$	$(G[7])$
1 0 0 1	$(S[2])$	$(S[3])$
1 0 1 0	$(S[4])$	$(S[5])$
1 0 1 1	$(S[6])$	$(S[7])$
1 1 0 0	$(G[0])$	$(R[3])$
1 1 0 1	$(G[2])$	$(G[3])$
1 1 1 0	$(G[4])$	$(G[5])$
1 1 1 1	$(G[6])$	interrupt

*Position 0 is that of the most significant bit
† Last operator Carry Out
‡ Last carry from operator 1 positions

3.4.2 Sequential Addressing

This type of addressing is basically that adopted for conventional instructions. Except in the case of branching, successive microinstructions are stored in successive command store locations, addressing being achieved by incrementation. Here we see that in the event of a sequential flow the next address part of the microinstruction is unused. In this situation the next address field may be used for other purposes, storing a constant for example. The idea of using a 'shared field' can be particularly useful in microprogramming and we shall return to it later.

Size of the Next Address Function   The 360-30 example showed that the next address function comprises a relatively large number of bits. In computers having a large command store (4 to 8 k words), the next address part generally involves less bits than would be necessary to address the whole store. However, in smaller machines with 512 to 2048 command store words, it is not unusual for the next address part to exceed the number of bits necessary to address the entire store.

   Note   At circuit level, the concept of a test occupying a time step as occurs in normal programming, no longer exists. Let us suppose that a choice must be made between two possible actions instigated by the two command signals C_1 and C_2 and depending on the value of a simple boolean variable V. A possible circuit is shown in figure 3.14 and, provided the bistable is loaded with the variable V before the

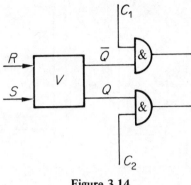

Figure 3.14

C_1/C_2 choice is made, no separate time step is required for the decision.

3.4.3 Sub-microprograms

It is quite common for a microprogram A to call a second micro-program B as a 'sub-microprogram'. For example, this might be the case for a SIN microprogram, which then uses multiplication as a sub-micro-program. As in normal programming the return to A has to be organised and this is conveniently achieved by furnishing B with a return address. In addition, B must know that it was entered by a call from another microprogram, a condition which if set into a flag bistable may be tested by B at the end of its execution. The most natural arrangement is to provide a register R to hold the return address and a bistable Q that will be set to 1 at the time of the transfer to B. At the last instruction of B, Q is tested and, if $Q = 1$, the address register of the micro-command store is loaded with the contents of R. If $Q = 0$, B will return to a more general microprogram (for example, the fetch phase of the next instruction or a sequence for storing results). Note that before returning control to A program, B resets Q to zero.

3.4.4 Acceleration of Branches

We shall analyse the functioning of the read-only store and its associated circuits as a synchronous finite-state machine. Let the microcommands be represented as the outputs S, and the address register as the state Q of the system. Let us take M_t as the general state of the machine execution network at the end of cycle t (basically equivalent to the condition codes at the beginning of cycle $t + 1$). M_t

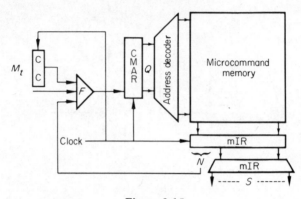

Figure 3.15

may be used for simple operations such as setting a C MAR bit at the
end of cycle t (function F of figure 3.15) and it must be available by
the beginning of cycle $t + 1$. Calling N the next address part of mIR, the
conventional model of figure 3.15 yields the two equations

$$S_t = f(Q_{t-1})$$

and

$$Q_{t-1} = g(Q_{t-2}, N_{t-2}, M_{t-3})$$

From these relationships it is apparent that if a branch takes place in
the microprogram following the result of an action in cycle t, the
machine must wait until cycle $t + 3$ before making the branch.

We can see that it is possible to accelerate branches if intermediate
storing of the function F in the address register is avoided and if the
corresponding circuit is included in the address decoding network. To
achieve this, the address decoding network may be preceded by a
combinational network called a modifier (figure 3.16).

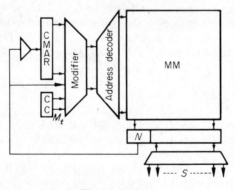

Figure 3.16

The functioning of the system is now governed by a relationship of the type

$$S_t = f(Q_{t-1}, N_t - 2, M_t - 2)$$

In order to accelerate further the execution of microprograms involving repeated local decisions, the aim is to obtain an operation described by a formula of the following type

$$S_t = f(Q_{t-1}, N_t - 2, M_{t-1})$$

This applies in the case of division algorithms, which have the property that at each step an addition or a subtraction must be made depending on whether the previous addition/subtraction has yielded a positive or negative result.

The above formula can be obtained by avoiding the intermediate processing of the condition codes as shown in figure 3.17.

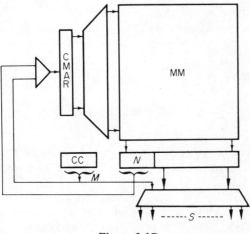

Figure 3.17

The structural development outlined above is essentially using the general principle that causes should be brought closer to their effects. This philosophy is frequently used in practice and current realisations are often a mixture of all three models, though there is particular emphasis on the structures of figures 3.16 and 3.17.

3.4.5 Addressing by Shift Register

Until now we have assumed that the addressing of the microinstruction store was achieved by decoding an address stored in an address register, the address being pure binary representation of the chosen word wire.

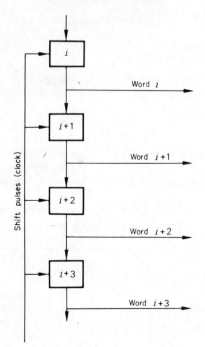

Figure 3.18

However, provided the microprogram involves few branches, it can be advantageous to use an alternative shift-register form of addressing circuit.

Let i, $i+1$, $i+2$, ... be successive outputs of this register (figure 3.18). If during time t, position i has the value 1 (and the other outputs are 0), word i can be selected at the same time as the input to cell $i+1$ is stimulated. The output of cell $i+1$ will consequently have the value 1 during time $t+1$, thus selecting word $i+1$, etc. (The shift register can be assumed to be constructed using D-type bistables.)

Obviously this over-simplified model must be refined to allow for conditional branching.

Figure 3.19 shows an example in which we have drawn together some of the principal properties of this type of addressing. The shift-register bistables are D0, D1, D2, D3, ... with the corresponding microinstruction words M0, M1, M2, M3, ... Timing is provided by the successive cycles T0, T1, T2, ..., microinstruction M0 being read during cycle T0. The figure in brackets after each word represents the cycle during which the word is read.

The operation is as follows. Assume all bistables are reset to 0, except for D0 which is initially set to 1.

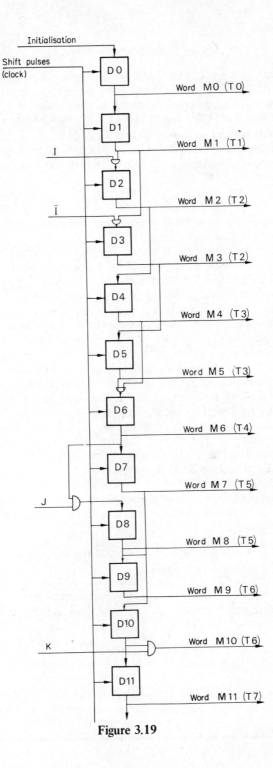

Figure 3.19

During cycle T0, word M0 is read and the command to switch bistable D1 to 1 is given. At this point the initialisation signal is 0 which means that during cycle T1, D0 will be reset to 0.

During cycle T1, word M1 is read and, depending on whether signal I is 1 or 0, control will pass to words M2 or M3.

During cycle T2, either word M2 or M3 will be read depending on the state of I during cycle T1. M2 designates M4 as its successor while M3 designates M5. Thus, the value of I determines two possible sequences M1, M2, M4, . . . or M1, M3, M5, ... As a simplification we have assumed that both M4 and M5 designate the same successor M6 to be read during cycle T4. For this reason, the input function of D6 is the logical OR of outputs D4 and D5.

Word M6 designates two successors which are not mutually exclusive. In fact, word M7 will be read during cycle T5 and, if $J = 1$ during cycle T4, word M8 will also be read during T5. The reaction of the command store to having two words simultaneously selected rather depends on how the store has been built. However, the usual result is the two selected microinstructions to be combined using the OR function. The main feature of this type of addressing is that it allows for several words to be addressed at the same time, an impossibility with the classical method of address decoding. This simultaneous microinstruction addressing allows an overlap which can be the subject of conditional information and furthermore the word output from memory need not be stored in a single storage location.

During cycle T6 word M9 will be read as will word M10 if $K = 1$. The use of condition K is slightly different from that of condition J. Word M8 is read during cycle T5 if J has the value 1 during the preceding cycle T4. However, M10 is read during cycle T6, if $K = 1$ during that same cycle.

It seems therefore that the action of K is faster than that of J in terms of the flow of the microprogram. In fact this is somewhat illusory since

(1) J only has to be at 1 at the end of cycle T4 while K must take the value 1 during all of cycle T6.

(2) While the AND gates associated with J and K are logically identical, they have rather different electrical requirements. The J AND gate merely triggers a bistable but the K gate is required to drive a word line of the memory.

This type of addressing is used in the Illiac IV computer and we shall return to it later.

3.4.6 The Mechanism of a Conditional Break: Waiting Cycles

In order to explain the mechanism of the sequence break (that is, the branch), we will take the example shown in figure 3.20 (which uses the modifier technique first described in figure 3.16).

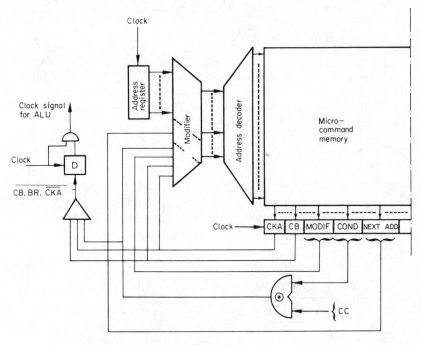

Figure 3.20

The reading and subsequent execution of a microinstruction are completed in two successive cycles, n and $n + 1$. We recall that reading during the course of cycle n involves the following procedure

(a) combination (by the modifier) of the contents of the address register, the state of the condition bistables and information from the next address field of the current microinstruction, to form the address of the microinstruction to be obeyed during time $n + 1$;

(b) selection of the word whose address is obtained from the modifier;

(c) loading of the microinstruction register.

Thus, in order for the break to take place in the course of cycle n, the conditional information must be known (and the corresponding signals available) at the beginning of the cycle. Where the information is

not available one cycle must elapse before the branching becomes
effective.

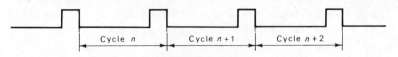

Figure 3.21

Let us assume that the sequence break condition is known in
advance; that is, it is not dependent on operations specified by the
break microinstruction itself. The condition is coded in microinstruction n and the break can be made immediately if the break
condition is satisfied (see figure 3.22a);

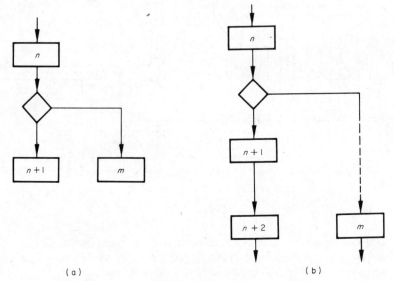

(a)   (b)

Figure 3.22

However if the break condition depends on the result of an
operation controlled by the break microinstruction n (figure 3.22b),
the conditional information will not be available until just before the
end of cycle n. It will therefore be impossible to read microinstruction
m in the course of this cycle, and it is therefore equally impossible to
execute m in cycle $n + 1$. As a result we have to suppress the ALU clock
pulse during cycle $n + 1$ for this type of branch.

To gain time, the next microinstruction in the unbranched sequence can be automatically read during cycle n (that is, without being modified by the modifier), in such a way as to avoid missing cycle n if no break occurs.

In the case where the branch condition is satisfied, the microinstruction register will contain the next microinstruction in sequence during cycle $n + 1$, though in fact this microinstruction must not be executed. In this situation the ALU clock pulse must be inhibited during cycle $n + 1$.

Consider again the schematic arrangement given in figure 3.20. Here the most-significant bits of the address are provided by the address register and the 4 least-significant bits are supplied by the next address field of the microinstruction. The CB (conditional break) field of the microinstruction indicates that the next address must be modified provided the condition in the COND field is satisfied. The arrangement is such that the modification only involves one of the 4 least-significant bits, the one in question being indicated by the MODIF field in figure 3.20.

The condition COND is compared with the state CC of the ALU. If the condition is satisfied (BR = 1) the next address bit specified by MODIF is complemented.

If the conditional information is obtained in advance, bit CKA takes the value 1. Alternatively if the condition is unknown until the completion of an operation controlled by the current microinstruction, CKA = 0.

If in fact a break occurs on a condition which is not known in advance, then CB.BR.$\overline{\text{CKA}}$ = 1, and the clock pulse sent to the ALU during cycle $n + 1$ must be suppressed. This is shown using a D-bistable (unit delay) in figure 3.20.

3.5 Timing — Delay Function

A microinstruction's execution time will depend on both the microinstruction itself and possibly the condition bistables. As will be appreciated the control circuits must know how long to wait before starting the following microinstruction, a time period determined by the delay function. The provision of such a function becomes particularly important for situations where the operations specified by the microinstruction vary in their duration. For example, an addition operation where the sum of two registers is placed in an accumulator is much shorter than a read or write operation involving the main store. In practice the delay function operates by indicating the point in time when the command store address register is updated (that is, clocked).

Various types of microinstruction timing are possible and we shall examine three typical examples.

3.5.1 Fixed Timing

When the timing is fixed a microinstruction takes place at each clock pulse. This assumes that the functioning times of the various parts of the machine are fixed and known, and, at the risk of a wasteful safety margin, are expressed in an integral number of cycles of the microinstruction store. For example, if a main-store read lasts three cycles of the command store, it is important to allow the appropriate time to elapse before subsequent microinstructions can include processing of the word extracted from the memory. Such a mode of operation has the advantage that the microinstruction word contains no special part relating to the timing, and the delay function is therefore implicit. On the other hand, the writing of microprograms is more complicated and can even lead to the provision of delay microinstructions during which nothing happens.

Furthermore in the course of the development of a computer, a fixed timing strategy makes it much more difficult to adopt a new and faster main store. This problem stems from the fact that a faster store would necessitate rewriting both the microinstruction sequences involving the main store and probably most other sequences, since there is the risk of the addresses being disordered.

3.5.2 Variable Synchronised Timing: the Holding Micro-order

With variable synchronised timing the command circuits remain very strictly under the control of the clock. When the microprogram waits for the result of an operation before continuing, the command circuits are momentarily interrupted (by inhibiting the command circuit clock) until the required condition is achieved.

As far as the command network is concerned the execution circuits (ALU, memory, etc.) are asynchronous, since they are stimulated at the start of a clock cycle and do not reply until their operations are complete. For example, the time interval which must elapse while waiting for the main store can be provided using a conditional micro-order (or delay function) such as: 'inhibit the clock pulse to the ALU and the command network until the store has recovered'. A micro-order of this kind is termed a 'holding micro-order'. Reading of the command store would then recommence at the first clock pulse arriving after the 'ready' signal has been emitted by the main store.

Generally speaking the delay function specifies one of several alternative conditions C_1, C_2, C_3 , ... Until the specified condition is realised the clock pulse is inhibited from both the command network and the execution networks which it controls (see figure 3.23 which shows a microcommand store *without* an output register). In this way a large part of the computer is immobilised (subject to certain con-

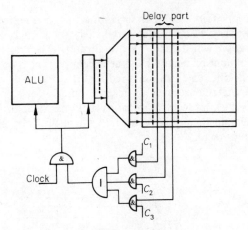

Figure 3.23

ditions) though some subsidiary functions continue to operate and to send signals to the control unit and its associated equipment (for example, signals setting interrupt registers).

3.5.3 Variable Advance. Delay Elements

Delay elements can be subdivided into two types, either with or without memory.

Delay Element Without Memory This is a device, with input S and output Q, designed to produce a simple delay function of the type produced by a delay line

$$Q_t = S_{t-\tau}$$

Delay Element with Memory As in the previous example this element exhibits a delay of τ seconds before the output changes to 1. In this case however the output remains in the 1 state until the element is reset by an input R

$$Q_t = \bar{R}_\theta \wedge (S_{t-\tau} \vee Q)$$

$$\forall \theta \; t > \theta > t - \tau$$

A delay element is made to correspond to each micro-command, the delay being chosen to be slightly greater than the maximum execution time of the corresponding micro-command. As shown in figure 3.24 the delay is selected by the 'delay function' part of the microinstruction word and the chosen delay is initiated at the same time as the microinstruction is extracted from the read-only memory. If the microinstruction itself comprises several parallel micro-operations, it is desirable that they all last for approximately the same time, since the longest operation will dictate the overall delay. Generally, all micro-instructions of approximately the same execution time specify the same delay element. Thus one can use a reduced number of delay elements, provided these circuits recover sufficiently quickly for a given delay to be utilised by two consecutive microinstructions. Such an arrangement is shown diagrammatically in figure 3.24 where the delay elements are of the 'without memory' type.

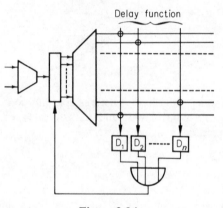

Delay function

Figure 3.24

Rather than have the microinstruction specify a particular time delay, an interesting alternative is to provide individual timing for each micro-operation. In this way the microinstruction specifies a set of micro-operations each of which is associated with a particular timing circuit, and the microinstruction is not considered finished until all of the component delays are complete. A circuit which detects the situation where all component delays have terminated and then allows the updating of the command memory address register (to initiate the next microinstruction) is shown in figure 3.25. This circuit, which uses the 'with memory' delay elements carries out a comparison between the sub-word specifying the delay elements and the outputs of the delay elements themselves.

Note   Throughout section 3.5 we have stopped the operation of the command network by removing the clock pulse from the address register of the command memory. This approach has enabled us to generalise the description to include the rather unusual situation where the command memory has no output register. However where such a register exists its clock pulse (like that of the address register) may be used to suspend the functioning of the command network.

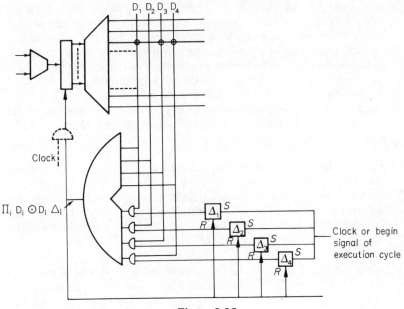

Figure 3.25

3.6 Check Bits

There are two basic types of check bit.

(a) Redundancy bits for the microinstruction word itself, there being at least one parity bit. However there can be several extra bits, increasing the possibilities of detecting or even correcting errors on the microinstruction word.

(b) Bits allowing supervisory calculations on the execution units thus providing facilities for the diagnosis of faults in these units.

Although there are no principles sufficiently widespread to warrant a detailed discussion, the importance of this part of the microinstruction word is emphasised by noting that the IBM 360-30 reserves some 14 bits for diagnostic functions.

3.7 Reduction in Size of the Microprogram Memory

The main means of reducing the size of the microprogram memory, at least so far as the number of words are concerned, is the interleaving of microprograms by establishing as many common sequences as possible. Some 'tricks of the trade' are mentioned below.

Bit Steering   An example should serve to explain bit steering. In the IBM 360-50 there is an I/O mode during which the central unit in conjunction with its buses, its operand registers and its ALU, is used to control certain channel multiplexing functions. When the machine is in this mode, certain micro-orders change their significance. The machine must first establish that it is in the I/O mode; this condition is then used to interpret the micro-orders, thereby complicating their decoding and necessitating a considerable increase in hardware. However, the length of the microinstructions is notably diminished and the bits of the microinstruction word are used in a more efficient manner.

State Bistable   The search for common sequences is often simplified by allowing certain branches to be delayed. In this context state bistables are very useful. Rather than branching as soon as conditional information is available, the condition is itself recorded in a 'state bistable'. This allows a 'trap' several cycles later, and may avoid the duplication of microinstructions before the trap occurs.

Loop Counter   It is often advantageous to provide a hardware register to act as a counter for microprogram loops. Thus, when a cycle must be repeated n times it is only necessary to write the microinstructions in the loop once, rather than n times. The loop counter can be initialised at $-n$ and incremented after each pass of the loop, an exit from the loop being made when the counter becomes zero. (Obviously the zero condition on the counter must generate a usable signal.)

Shared Fields   A shared field is a microinstruction field that can be used as an item of information. As such it is capable of being connected to the ALU to intervene in calculations, thus increasing the possibilities for interpretation of the microinstruction. For example, the shared field can be combined with the condition codes in order to generate an address to be sent into the address register of the read-only store.

Nanoprogramming   This rather inappropriately named term is used in connection with the mechanism described below (see ref. 19).
   We shall consider the case of a microinstruction word of 100 bits. It is certain that the 2^{100} possible words will not be used and generally only a very much reduced subset will be required. Let us suppose that only $1024 = 2^{10}$ combinations are used. The idea then is to store a microprogram not as a sequence of microinstructions but as a sequence of pointers to the microinstructions, each pointer allowing access to one of the 1024 microinstructions. A first store, called the 'control store', contains the pointers and a second store, the 'nano store', memorises the microinstructions. In our example, let us suppose that the set of microprograms amounts to 2000 words. The control store will thus have $2000 \times 10 = 20\ 000$ bits. (We recall that the control store

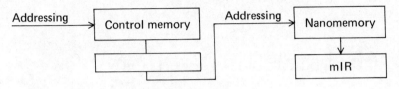

Figure 3.26

simply contains pointers to the nano store and its words are therefore of length $10 = \log_2 1024$.) The nano store, containing the micro-instructions actually used, has 1024 words of 100 bits (that is, approximately 100 000 bits) giving a total of $20\,000 + 100\,000 = 120\,000$ bits. Thus a saving of 40 per cent is obtained compared with a single 'level' control store which would have $2000 \times 100 = 200\,000$ bits.

4 Instruction Repertoire and Microprogramming

Microprogramming can be considered from two points of view. First, there is that of the hardware designer, whose objective is the definition and realisation of a repertoire of instructions. To use common terminology, this is the 'hardware' point of view. The circuit designer therefore sees in microprogramming a solution to the technical and economic difficulties in endowing a machine with an adequate repertoire of instructions.

Second, there is the 'higher level' view, directed more towards the realisation of established languages and the problems of simulation, or emulation, of other machines. This 'software' approach both tends to accentuate the possibilities of efficient interpretation, and exploit the possibilities of low-level algorithms that are offered by micro-programming.

A microprogrammed computer's instruction set will include the basic instructions of addition, multiplication, conditional jump, etc. (often with several formats of operands) but in addition it may be enriched with more sophisticated instructions. The latter can be complex data operations such as ARC SIN, change of coordinate axes, table look-up, table updating, sorting, etc.

Alternatively complex instructions can perform operations relating several independent sub-programs to one another, and they therefore assume the role of procedures normally associated with a supervisory program. Examples are the subroutine call (without supervisor inter-vention), interrupt handling, etc.

4.1 Choice between Wired and Stored Microprogram Control

For given external characteristics (reliability, calculation speed, instruc-tion set, etc.) the choice between wired control and stored micro-program control can be made by comparing the respective costs of each solution.

Figure 4.1 shows the cost as a function of the richness of the instruction repertoire. The concept of 'richness' of a repertoire of instructions is not easily quantifiable but its meaning is generally fairly clear if we take into account the field of application for which the

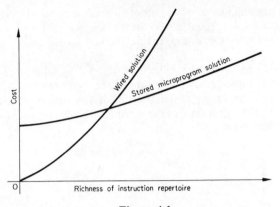

Figure 4.1

computer is intended. In fact, even when a computer is said to be general-purpose, it is frequently used for a quite specific sphere of application. Its potential market is generally known and restricted, and its selling price and basic software are tailored accordingly.

From figure 4.1 it will be noted that after a fairly heavy initial investment, the cost of implementation by stored microprograms increases slowly. This is understandable since initial investment must be made in a special memory to contain the microprograms. However, adding an extra instruction only amounts to adding a few corresponding microinstruction words and this is true even for relatively complex instructions like an ARC SIN. (The ARC SIN microprogram could call existing microprograms, such as those for multiplication or division.) On the other hand, in a wired solution it is frequently necessary to provide a special hardware operator for an operation such as ARC SIN.

It is difficult to compare wired and microprogrammed approaches. Nevertheless, most designers agree that somewhere between 8 and 16 bits of ROM can be used to replace a gating function. Note also that a standard 16-lead package involves a total implementation cost of about $1.00 (of which approximately 30 cents are accounted for in packaging). Equally, the total cost for one bit of ROM is about 1 cent, using a 4096 bit ROM package.

The crossover region of figure 4.1 is rather difficult to establish and appreciation of this point remains the province of the experienced design engineer. In practice, a number of imponderable factors have to be taken into account: these include the available experience in a given field; the cost and time needed to perfect the prototype; the customer's preferences for one solution or another; the acceptability of certain optional devices and the fact that their adoption by many customers will lower the unit costs.

Microprogramming is often adopted because it allows designers to use a methodical approach, and hence the possibility of reasonably accurate cost estimates during the design, verification and development phases.

A high initial cost is exhibited in figure 4.2a where the cost per instruction is indicated as a function of the number of instructions in the repertoire. It causes the initial fall of the curves, which reach a minimum and then increase as the word length and complication of the decoding circuits increases.

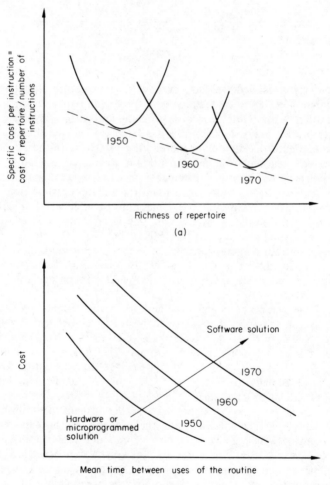

Figure 4.2

Figure 4.2b illustrates the considerations that have to be taken into account for realising a routine by hardware rather than software. In this context 'routine' means a piece of microprogramming which apart from its beginning and end has little contact with other parts of the system. It receives input parameters and gives a result. For such a routine to be worth realising by microprogramming it should be reasonably time consuming (that is, inefficient in normal software) and frequently used.

Effectively, microprogramming is being used as a way of providing hardware routines; the trend is to have more and more 'hardware' routines in the repertoire, and microprogramming is the easiest way to produce them. Routines implemented in this way are frequently referred to as 'firmware'.

4.2 Rich Code and Inexpensive Machines

It is possible, even without microprogramming, to provide a small computer with quite a rich repertoire of interpretive instructions. In assembly, these interpretive instructions are transformed into subroutine calls which, when they are executed, result in a loss of performance. Microprogramming can be defined as the in-building of such subroutines in specialised memories. The gain in performance arises primarily from the greater operating speed of the memories used and from the fact that all the fetch phases of the instructions are saved.

As discussed in detail in chapter 3 the length and structure of the microprogram word is designed to suit the computer resources being controlled. For example, a small or medium-sized computer can be provided with a rich instruction code similar to that of a much more powerful machine. Thus the small computer is compatible with the large machine (upward compatability), in that programs written for the small computer are acceptable to the large machine. As a consequence a whole range of compatible machines can be designed, a good example being the IBM 360 series.

4.3 Microprogramming in Large Machines

For the purposes of this section, we shall categorise a large machine as having a flow of information of at least 10^6 to 10^7 bits per second on the main memory bus.

In large machines, microprogramming may be considered from two very different points of view.

(1) First, microprogramming provides a means of implementing the control logic, and providing both the basic and sophisticated instructions necessary for the computer operation. The flexibility of

microprogramming is such that even small 'classic programs' can be microprogrammed, some examples being the handling of interrupts, simple loading routines, and programs for testing and fault diagnosis.

(2) The second facet of microprogramming, that of being an architectural tool is a more recent innovation. One of the pioneers in this field is the Standard Computer Corporation whose computers are distinguished by their so called 'inner computer' structure, which will be examined in chapter 5.

In large computers, such as the IBM 360-85, microprogramming is generally only used to bring about the execution phase of instructions; functions such as the fetch phase (or the expected fetch), the management of the instruction counter and the precoding of the instructions (to prepare jump instructions, for example) usually being hard-wired. In machines of this sort the instruction fetching unit and the execution unit are thus relatively independent in their operation.

4.3.1 Use of Microprogramming in the Illiac IV*

It is interesting to quote the introductory sentence of a recent paper describing the microprogramming of the Illiac IV† computer: 'Because of its high speed operation, large instruction repertoire and centralised control, the Illiac IV computer uses a read-only memory (ROM) to translate the instructions into control enables.' This is an important statement since it contradicts the fairly widespread view that microprogramming implies slowness of operation. The sentence contains a little more, since it specifies a ROM rather than a writable memory. Also, it will be noted that, according to the authors of the Illiac IV project, the richness and complexity of the instruction repertoire (260 instructions, various operand formats) justifies the use of microprogramming.

A better understanding of the instruction flow of this unusual computer can be gained by referring to figure 4.3. Here the control unit of the Illiac IV is depicted as a series of modules, through which the instructions are sequentially processed.

(1) ILA – Instruction Look Ahead – extracts blocks of sixteen contiguous instructions from the stores associated with the processing units and stores them in a first-in first-out queue (FIFO).

(2) ADVAST – Advanced Station – receives instructions from ILA

---

*A description of the Illiac IV can be found in D. L. Slotnick, 'Computer Structures' in *Architecture and Design of Computers* (ed. G. Boulaye), Dunod, Paris, 1971.
†'Use of microprogramming in Illiac IV,' Grenoble workshop on microprogramming, 1970; or H. J. White and E. K. C. Yu, 'Use of read-only memory in Illiac IV', A.F.I.P.S. Conf. Proc. 36, *S.J.C.C.*, 1970, 197–205.

and organises preprocessing operations such as address arithmetic and indexing or interrupt processing. From the instructions thus prepared, ADVAST produces a 'final queue' (FINQ) which is also of the first-in first-out type.

In order to simplify the work of ADVAST the instructions are divided into two classes: CU instructions and PE instructions. CU instructions produce local operations in the control unit (jumps,

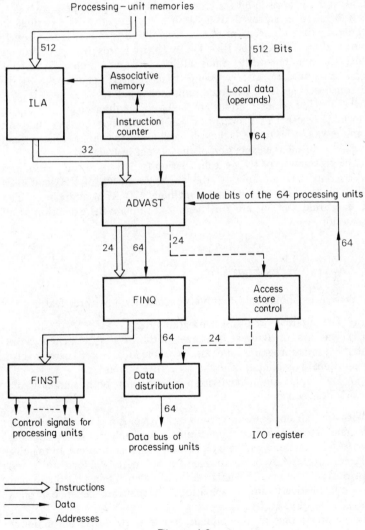

Figure 4.3

indexes, etc) while PE instructions control the operation of the processing units. ADVAST is entirely responsible for processing CU instructions but is only partly concerned with PE instructions, which it 'preprocesses' before transmitting them to FINST (final station).

(3) FINST receives the instructions sent by ADVAST via FINQ and organises the execution phase of each instruction.

The module FINST is microprogrammed. It uses a discrete component read-only store with 720 words of 280 bits, the cycle time being 50 ns, and the word-to-bit coupling is of the transistor type.

Addressing is achieved using a shift register and, as described in chapter 3, this arrangement allows several words to be simultaneously addressed. In effect, in the Illiac IV, up to five words per instruction are addressed simultaneously. Since additionally two compatible instructions can operate at the same time, FINST allows up to 10 microinstructions to be executed simultaneously.

In FINST, two instructions are analysed simultaneously in order to determine whether their execution can take place at the same time. An example would be. to see if the call on data for the next instruction can take place during the execution of the current instruction.

The pre-analysis of the next instruction to determine the possibilities for overlap uses an area of the ROM consisting of 250 addresses called the overlap section. The remaining 470 ROM addresses, called the execution section, are sufficient to complete the execution of all instruction types.

4.3.2 Specialised Processing Units

The present technological situation is characterised by three features

(a) The intensive use of microprogramming.

(b) The use of integrated stores, both for the permanent store containing microprograms, and for a writable local store. There are also the additional possibilities of using associative memories.

(c) The rapid commercialisation of LSI for both standard and specially designed circuits.

With the current state of technology, systems and circuit designers have much more scope for innovation; for example, they may consider new modules or units with which to build their computers. In the past designers have usually been confined to arithmetic and logic units, and input/output modules. The latter are often elementary and the former carry out relatively simple operations, as they are dependent on a 'central' control unit.

In contrast, one of the present trends is to devise autonomous operations, each provided with their own control unit. For this 'decentralised' form of control to be viable, the operations being controlled should be as independent as possible. Also the initiation of these operations should be short when compared with the duration of the processes they control.

Such a module, called a *processor*, can be characterised by an algorithm. To merit a specialised processor, an algorithm should have the following characteristics

(1) Frequent use. This is obvious; otherwise a simple subroutine could be used in place of the processor.

(2) Relatively simple data flowchart. The process should be relatively self-contained, having little connection with the remainder of the system. In other words a routine which, once initiated, will proceed without reference to what may be happening elsewhere in the computer. It is this feature which allows the corresponding processor to be made autonomous.

(3) Potentially time-consuming. The overall computing efficiency may benefit very considerably if a potentially time-consuming routine can be realised in a special purpose processor − for example, routines requiring frequent calls to be made on the main store. As an example we shall briefly illustrate such a processor.

The Sort Processor*   Let us consider records that have been organised in the form of (information-key) pairs. In general, sorting consists of arranging the records so that their key words form an ordered sequence.

The process of sorting can be subdivided into two main phases

(1) Creation of ordered subsets called blocks. For example, from the following keys

$$1-3-8-2-4-9-7-0-18-21-29-14-17-55$$

the blocks (represented by their keys) might be formed as follows

$$1-3-8 \quad 2-4-9 \quad 7 \quad 0-18-21-29 \quad 14-17-55$$

(2) Merging. Two blocks recorded in two sequential access storage media (magnetic discs or tapes) are merged together to form a single block. This process is repeatedly applied to block pairs until, ultimately, only one large block remains. The two blocks to be merged are examined simultaneously and the keys from each block are

---

*This processor was first presented by H. Barsamian in 'Firmware sort processor with LSI components', *S.J.C.C.*, 1970, pp. 183–90. Incidentally, this processor illustrates the complementary aspects of microprogramming and LSI technology. For sort algorithms see ACM Communications, May 1963, which reports a symposium on the subject.

compared. For example, blocks 1–3–8 and 2–4–9 become block
1–2–3–4–8–9 following the procedure illustrated below.

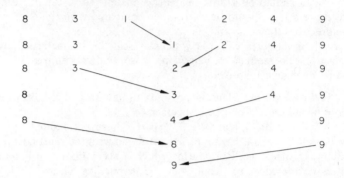

The blocks are produced from data in the main store, while their
merging into one, which is achieved with the aid of magnetic tapes or
discs, involves the use of input/output procedures. In effect, the sorting
unit forms a small autonomous processor within the main computer
which is dedicated to ordering blocks derived from the main store.

Figure 4.4 gives a block diagram of the sort processor and shows an
associative memory SM containing (key, record-address) pairs, a register
RF which is the input/output register for the processor, and a
microprogram store.

The sort processor connects to the remainder of the computer via
the main memory bus, and the data flow and main memory allocation
are illustrated in figure 4.5.

The CPU activates the sort processor by giving it a start signal, to
indicate that the control word currently on the main memory bus

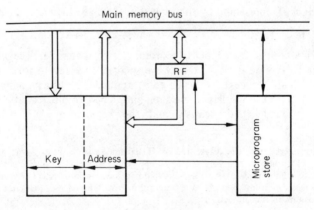

Figure 4.4

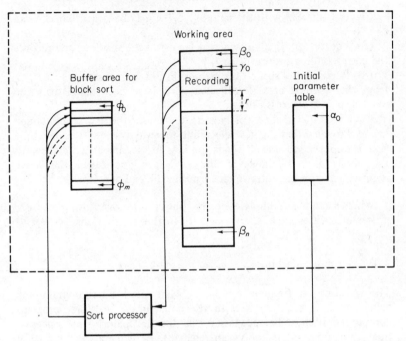

Figure 4.5

contains the following information

(a) the nature of the sort, for example, whether ascending or descending;

(b) address α_0 of the 'initial parameter table' which contains the following information:

(i) addresses β_0 and β_n of the first and last records of the working area;

(ii) address γ_0 of the key of the first record;

(iii) length l of this key;

(iv) record length r (in this case all records are assumed to be of the same length).

The table of parameters also contains the description of the buffer area allocated to the processor for the formation of a block sort — for example, the starting and finishing addresses θ_0 and θ_n of the buffer area.

After receiving the control word, the sort processor proceeds in the following manner

(1) From the initial parameters, it calculates the starting addresses β_i of the records and of their keys K_i, $i = 0,1,2,\ldots n$.

(2) Fills the SM with the pairs $\{K_i, \beta_i\}$ (n may be larger than the size of SM).

(3) Locates the first key K_0 (the largest or the smallest) and records the corresponding address β_0 in θ_0.

(4) Replaces the space thus created in SM with the next pair K_j, β_j from the working area. If all such pairs have been taken from the working area the sort is finished.

(5) Finds the smallest (or largest) key among the new set contained in SM. Provided that the key selected in this way is larger (smaller) than that previously selected, it sends the key and its associated address to the buffer area. If, however, the key does not satisfy the above requirement, the last entry in fact signifies the end of a block sort.

When sorting is complete or the buffer area overflows, the sort processor notifies the CPU and waits for further instructions.

4.4 Amorphous Machines

The question is frequently asked: 'what does microprogramming achieve that is basically new to the concept of the stored-program computer?' It must be recognised that for the majority of concepts, microprogramming is only an element of general technological progress. At the same time, it seems that the concept of the amorphous machine is completely new, and that is has been brought about by microprogramming. (Some embryonic traces of this new concept can be seen in certain stored logic devices of second generation machines.)

With an amorphous machine the user can specify the instruction repertoire that he wants by writing his own microprograms and to simplify this process the microinstructions are basically of the instruction type. Moreover, certain aids are available to the user and these almost always include a microprogram simulator.

4.5 Some Notes on Miniprogramming

Microprogramming can be regarded as the lowest of three programming levels

(a) programming in a high level language (Fortran, Algol, PL/1 or a language specially adapted for the computer);
(b) programming in assembly language;
(c) microprogramming.

Consider for example a small computer intended to serve as a scheduler or industrial-process controller. The program will probably be relatively short and will remain practically unchanged during the life of the computer. Thus to preserve the two levels, of assembly language and of microprogramming, appears rather wasteful. It seems that to have a single intermediate level, involving a repertoire of mini-instructions might allow greater flexibility and improved efficiency. In practice it requires a great deal of care and a certain taste for detail to write a program in this form of language. However, the programs are short and the engineers required to write them will generally have acquired the habit and taste for efficiency, even to the detriment of their peace of mind!

5 Microprogramming and Computer Structures

In the previous chapter we described the use of microprogramming as a method of implementing control logic and hence providing the required instruction set. Chapter 4 also suggested that microprogramming could be used as an architectural tool and it is this aspect that we will amplify in the present chapter. As the architectural implications of microprogramming are relatively new (*post* 1968), consideration must be given to the interrelation of microprogramming and the current trends in computer structures. We shall therefore outline the general trends in the use of computers, and indicate the notable advances in technology. Subsequently, we shall consider how microprogramming can be used to exploit technology and thus improve the external characteristics of a computer.

5.1 System trends

The speed of logic circuits has increased roughly by a factor of 10 times per decade, as indicated in figure 5.1. Another interesting curve, shown in figure 5.2, demonstrates that from 1960 the price of logic elements has decreased by a factor of about 10 for every five years. A third graph, figure 5.3, shows how efficiency measured in terms of instructions per second has increased at a rate of about 10 times every five years. For the purpose of figure 5.3 the efficiency could be taken as the average operational history of a computer over one year, allowing for 'down time'.

The fact that the gain in performance is a factor of 10 over a five-year period while calculating speeds have only increased by an order of magnitude in a decade, is due to an accompanying improvement in the organisation of control and management systems within the computer. These 'systems' advances include interleaved memories, instruction overlap techniques, etc., and also the automation of tasks previously carried out manually, such as job chaining, resource allocation, interrupt handling, etc. Thus the improved performance is as much due to systems organisation as to technological advances.

The following distinctions and definitions are current

The *first generation* of computers constitutes computer 'prehistory' (machines built from tube and electromechanical relays).

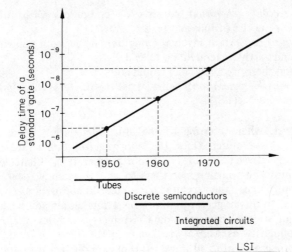

Figure 5.1

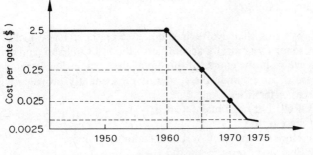

Figure 5.2

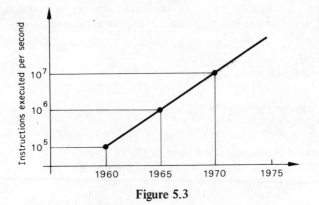

Figure 5.3

The *second generation* consists of computers with tubes and magnetic memories (drums and ferrite cores).

The *third generation* involves computers made from semiconductor circuits and partly integrated modules.

In addition there are many who would add:

The *fourth generation*, being those computers with large scale integrated circuits (LSI).

However, when referring to the fourth generation, a more subtle description is required since the above definitions afford no clear distinction between the third and fourth generations. Characterisation of the third and fourth generations by purely technological means is inadequate, since the architectural considerations are equally as important. In this respect, the third generation has already introduced a number of original concepts: data channels, computer families, software modularity as well as hardware in the form of status words, process-processors, etc.; all these concepts are distinct from the strictly technological point of view.

Which areas are system designers currently considering, in order to improve computer performance? The following list covers most of the more important areas

(a) Systems that evolve in the course of time. These include those which adapt dynamically according to the tasks in hand, and also those which evolve in the course of the life of the system. The latter would be the case if for example the system is subsequently provided with new resources or facilities.

(b) Reliability and maintenance.

(c) Ease of use.

(d) More general man—machine communications.

(e) Sharing of resources.

To take account of these requirements, hardware facilities must increase and improve, and as we have already seen the current technological situation is favourable to such an expansion.

5.2 Next Generation Computers

Some desirable hardware facilities to be expected in the next generation of computers include

(a) stack processing operations;
(b) memory updating with automatic addressing;

(c) complete initialisation;

(d) ultra-fast stores for pointers and lists; if possible, associative stores and processing units;

(e) list processing operations;

(f) file processing operations (we have already discussed sorting).

These hardware resources would simplify programming and improve data transfer times. There should also be better planning, in particular so far as operations facilitating supervision tasks are concerned. For example

(a) automatic interlocking between processors in a multiprocessor;

(b) fast local storage that can be addressed linearly or associatively, to contain the small internal program loops.

(c) locally autonomous input/output functions to reduce the number of central processor interruptions — for example, autonomous channels with direct memory access.

Moreover, the degree of automation attained at present means that the majority of operations are initialised by interrupt signals. As a result the manipulation and handling of interrupts becomes one of the most time-consuming tasks in a computer.

The problem of reducing interrupt processing time can be tackled in two ways. First by having (where possible) the information needed during the interrupt prepared before the interrupt occurs, thus reducing the duration of the interrupt itself. The second approach involves increased automation of interrupt handling, with particular emphasis on avoiding calls to the supervisor. In practice, a programmed structure greatly facilitates systematic handling of interrupts and this topic will be expanded in the following section.

5.3 Interrupt Handling

An interrupt is said to occur when a computer receives an interrupt request part way through the execution of a program. The interrupt request is activated by an interrupt signal and the resulting processing must

(a) ensure that the interrupted program can subsequently be resumed from the point at which the break was made;

(b) analyse the interrupt request and set the necessary actions in motion. When these actions are complete, the interrupted program must be resumed.

The basic fetch–execute loop, which is common to all instructions of a program, is shown below (see also figure 1.7 and the beginning of section 3.2).

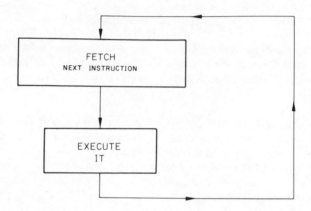

Program interruption consists of breaking the loop and since the status at the time of the break must be stored, the position of the break must be carefully chosen.

We shall defer the discussion of this choice until later and assume that the optimum position is after the EXECUTE phase. The flowchart then becomes

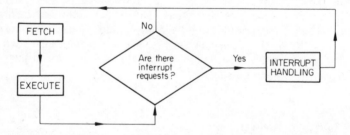

Generally, interrupts fall into two categories: internal and external. External interrupts are caused by events outside the computer and although the servicing time for such interrupts is generally fairly short, the delay before the program is interrupted must usually be less than some predetermined maximum.

A common example of external interrupts is seen in the situation where a signal is generated by a peripheral device to indicate that information, previously requested, is now available in the peripheral's buffer register. Another illustrative example of external interrupts can be taken from the field of real-time process control. In this case the computer monitors external signals, which characterise the state of the process under control. If these signals indicate that the process is entering a critical phase, an interrupt will be generated and corrective action will need to be taken, possibly to the exclusion of all other activities. A situation of this sort might well occur in a thermal power-plant which uses a computer to control its operation and optimise its output. All optimisation calculations must be stopped if an alarm signal indicates that an explosion is imminent somewhere in the plant and control must be given immediately to a program suited to this new situation.

An internal interrupt or 'trap', may be caused by an abnormal condition in the computer itself, or an unusual program-generated situation. Examples of the former include voltages outside tolerance, memory parity error, etc., and the latter program-generated traps could be caused by calculation overflow, use of non-existent or non-authorised instructions or attempts to use unavailable peripheral units. A more comprehensive list of traps is given below

(a) voltages outside tolerance;
(b) parity errors on the contents of a word read from main memory;
(c) attempts at writing or reading in a forbidden zone of the store;
(d) attempts to use instructions forbidden in the execution mode of the program (for example, an instruction reserved for the supervisor);
(e) attempts to use peripheral equipment forbidden or unavailable to the present user;
(f) use of non-existent instructions;
(g) movement of the internal clock to a value fixed in advance;
(h) fixed-point overflow;
(i) floating-point exponent overflow;
(j) floating-point exponent underflow;
(k) alignment faults in division;
(l) manual interruption from the console.

The interrupt status is recorded in an 'interrupt register', the bits of which correspond to each cause or class of interrupt and are set by the corresponding interrupt signals.

When several interrupts occur at the same time a hierarchical system of priorities is established to decide which interrupt is to be serviced first (such an arrangement is particularly important for handling external interrupts). In addition to interrupt priorities, a computer must have instructions for processing the contents of the interrupt register, plus the facility for masking (that is, ignoring) certain interrupt bits using an 'interrupt mask register'.

If ITR is the interrupt register and ITM is the interrupt mask register, processing is interrupted if $E\,i$

$$\exists i \quad (\text{ITR}\,[i]) \text{ AND } (\text{ITM}\,[i]) = 1$$

If this equation is satisfied, signal IT in figure 5.4 is set to 1 and a branch is made in the microprogram control.

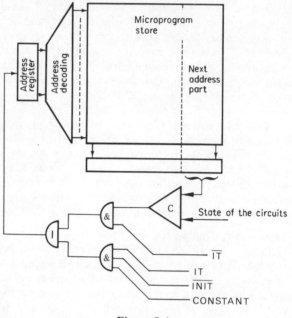

Figure 5.4

It is desirable to be able in inhibit the signal IT; hence the signal INIT which, if it has the value 1, performs this inhibition.

5.3.1 Effect of an Interrupt Signal on Microprogram Control: The Interrupt Mechanism

Referring to figure 5.4, in the absence of an interrupt, the next address is calculated in circuit C using the next address part of the micro-instruction and the state of the condition bistables.

In the case of a valid interrupt (signal INIT = 0), the next address calculation is replaced by the transmission of a constant. Hence the microprogram M1, currently being executed, is interrupted and another microprogram M2 is initialised.

If at the conclusion of M2, M1 is to be resumed from the point where the interrupt occurred, the first task of M2 is to store the status of M1, (that is, the contents of various registers and the prevailing modes of operation) that existed at the point in time when M1 was interrupted. In fact, the whole status of the machine must be preserved and this can be a major task.

It can be seen that similar principles apply when interrupting a microprogram as those that occur when an interrupt takes place during a normal program. For example, the interrupting microprogram stores the next address calculated by circuit C, in order to recall it at the end of the interruption.

At the same time, it should be noted that to interrupt a microprogram, or rather an instruction, in the process of its operation, can lead to the storing of quite a considerable amount of information. It is therefore important to choose the interruption point in such a way as to minimise this storage requirement. It is particularly desirable to interrupt a microprogram at the end of an instruction being processed. The interrupt can also be placed immediately after the fetch phase but before the start of the execution phase. In fact at these times it is only necessary to preserve the few registers associated with the program being run. This means that it is the status of the interrupted program that must be safeguarded, rather than the status of the machine. Nevertheless in certain cases the interruption at the end of the instruction being processed is not acceptable. The following are a few examples

(a) if the operation code to be executed is not recognised by the computer;

(b) if the operation code is forbidden in the current mode of operation;

(c) during a very lengthy operation.

An example of the latter is a multi-level indirect addressing where the interruption is made between two adjacent levels. Iterative instructions also tend to be very time consuming and examples include instructions to simulate 'associative' table searches or instructions involving the movement of complete areas of memory.

5.3.2 The Role of Interrupt Inhibition

We have just explained why the interrupt points should be chosen carefully. However, since the interrupt signal is external to the microprogram one cannot choose the moment when it arrives and therefore provision must be made for the microprogram to control the input of this signal. This is done simply by the setting of an inhibit bit, in other words the INIT signal referred to above and now shown in figure 5.5. This signal generally results from a bistable set at 1 or 0 by command from a microinstruction.

When an interrupt ITR $[i]$ switches to 1, it is considered active if it has not been masked by the program (or ultimately by the microprogram) and provided it has not been inhibited by the microprogram.

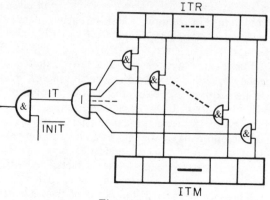

Figure 5.5

Thus there is an interrupt if

$$\exists i, \overline{\text{INIT}} = \text{ITR} \: [i] = \text{ITM} \: [i] = 1$$

or

$$\overline{\text{INIT}} \cdot \Sigma \: (\text{ITR} \: [i] \cdot \text{ITM} \: [i]) = 1$$

If this is the case, the next address is automatically the start address of the interrupt servicing microprogram M2.

Microprogram M2 must begin by inhibiting all interrupts of equal or lower priority than the one being handled. If the interrupt handling is simple it can be directly microprogrammed; however in more complex situations control may be passed to the supervisor.

5.4 Role of the Supervisor

The supervisor is the group of programs (and microprograms) which carry out the various operations necessary for the overall operation of the computer, namely the

   (a) linking or chaining of programs,
   (b) loading of programs,
   (c) input and handling of interrupts,
   (d) management of the main store or bulk memory, and
   (e) general management of computer resources.

5.5 Use of Microprogramming

Microprogramming modifies the extent to which the supervisor is used, and it does this in two different ways

(1) It allows for instructions which include supervisor operations in their own handling. An example is a sub-routine call in a system with dynamic store allocation, where the microprogram consults the table of subroutine start addresses without recourse to the supervisor.

(2) It effects certain simple and systematic operations which lend themselves to microprogramming. Some examples are

(a) linking or chaining of programs;

(b) interrupt recognition;

(c) handling of certain interruptions

   (i) voltage outside tolerance;

   (ii) floating point overflow;

   (iii) attempt at executing an operation code which is either protected or illegal;

   (iv) process synchronisation (for example, automatic internal signalling operations).

5.6 Role of Microprogramming in Computer Architecture; 'Inner Computer' Structure

At the beginning of this book, we presented microprogramming as a methodical and practical means of implementing the control logic of a computer. Subsequently in the second half of chapter 3 and in chapter 4, we saw how a microprogrammed control unit can increase efficiency by providing facilities such as good interruptibility, auto-repetition, and the nesting of subroutines. All these advances now allow microprogramming to be considered as an extension of software, in the sense that it becomes an efficient tool for organising a set of subroutines and controlling their execution. For example, we have noted that the skeleton of the basic supervisor could itself be microprogrammed to advantage. And we have further shown that certain standard and very individualised routines can also be microprogrammed.

Let us reconsider the structure of the computer outlined in chapter 1 as redrawn in figure 5.6.

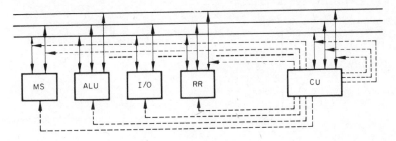

Figure 5.6

The different modules — main store MS, arithmetic and logic unit ALU, input/output unit I/O, registers or ultra-fast local store RR — and the control unit CU are all connected to the buses. There can be 1, 2, 3 or more buses and the more that are used, the greater the possibilities for simultaneous operation of computer resources. Microprogramming, especially field-structural microprogramming, allows these possibilities to be exploited to the full.

The control unit CU sends command signals to the other modules and establishes the connections between modules by controlling the bus connections. In order to achieve the two-way flow suggested by figure 5.6 it is necessary to have the command signals themselves relayed by a bus (figure 5.7); that is, to use an 'order bus' to transmit command signals to the processing boxes. The order bus is divided into two sub-buses: one carrying a label saying which processing box is addressed; the other specifying the commands. All modules compare the label-bus with their own locally stored name and if the name matches, the processing module accepts the order and carries out the required operation. A well-known example of this type of structure is the DEC PDP 11 computer.

Using figures 5.6 and 5.7, we can explain the use of micro-programming as a tool for the structuring of computers. There are two possible approaches

(1) To emphasise the structure suggested by figure 5.7 and try to put into each processing module the parts of the microprogram relating to that module. This avoidance of the control unit represents a further move towards modularity; that is, one buys a processing module and the set of instructions relating to that module. Here the control unit sees its role reduced to operations such as 'FETCH an instruction', 'Give control to a module' and 'Go to further steps when an addressed

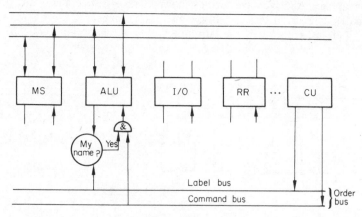

Figure 5.7

module has completed its work'. (For example, see the PB 6 scheduler made by Merlin-Gerin.)

(2) In the structure shown in figure 5.6, if the CU is microprogrammed, which is increasingly the case, it becomes almost a small computer in its own right. Almost that is, since it still has to use the ALU to carry out certain calculations which are necessary for its operation. If we provide the CU with its own ALU it becomes a complete, albeit rather elementary computer, with its own microprogram store, fast registers and calculation circuits.

In order to produce an effective computer, we must match the capabilities of the various modules (MS, ALU, I/O, etc.) and consequently provide a relatively autonomous machine. Other functional modules can be added to the classic modules. an example being the sort processor, described in the previous chapter.

The exchanges between functional modules (which are so many specialised processors) not only diminish, but also are no longer satisfied with the rigid framework of direct links via buses. For example, the format of the units of information transmitted between units can vary or intermediate operations may prove necessary. Being relieved of the need to ensure microscopic control the CU is concerned with macroscopic control and can handle these intermediate operations. Such a development leads to the structure shown in figure 5.8 in which all the processors communicate with one another via the central control unit. The CU is thus a computer within a computer and is frequently referred to as an 'inner computer'. A commercial example of an inner computer structure is seen in the IC 4000 and IC 7000 machines produced by the Standard Computer Corporation in the United States.

In studying computer structures we should appreciate that architectural development must be accompanied by improvements in the understanding of software concepts. One fact is becoming increasingly evident: every program is an assembly of subroutines, and computers will become more efficient if their structures take this fact into account.

The role and characteristics of the inner computer emerge as follows

(1) Its instruction repertoire must be designed to facilitate the organisation of subroutines: calls, cascaded calls, links, etc.

(2) It must be very fast (therefore quite small) and certain routines or subroutines that are used very frequently must be retained in the inner computer's memory.

(3) To meet the processors' needs for flexibility and efficiency in use, programming of the inner computer is in fact microprogramming. To facilitate their use, these instructions are of the mini-instruction type (which we have also called 'instruction-type microinstructions').

(4) The inner computer has a read–write memory that can be

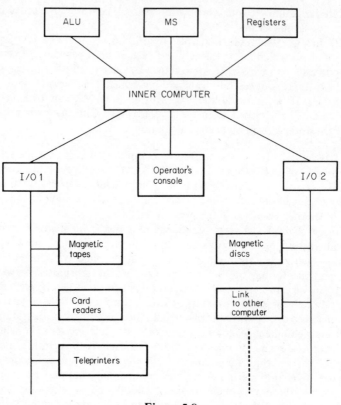

Figure 5.8

reloaded either from the main store or via the I/O units, a facility which allows dynamic modification and development of the system.

These different characteristics make the inner computer a remarkable tool for the emulation of other machines.

5.6.1 Constituent Parts of the SCC IC 7000 Inner Computer

Figure 5.9 shows the main components, which are

(a) a mini-arithmetic and logic unit, involving an 11-bit adder;
(b) registers of 11 and 16 bits;
(c) a store of 1024 words of 36 bits, cycle time 1 μs. A storage word contains either 36 data bits or two microinstructions of 18 bits each;
(d) the translator;

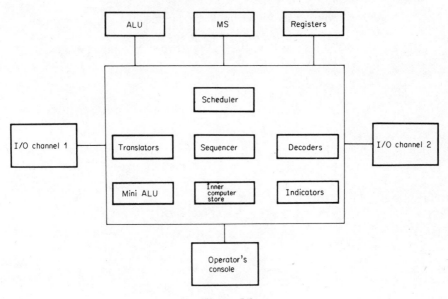

Figure 5.9

(e) the scheduler;
(f) the sequencer.

The latter three elements are needed for the interpretive functioning of the computer.

The scheduler is a hard-wired unit which directs the interrupts as a function of their priorities. When several interrupt requests occur together they are arranged in the form of a queue. However, when no interrupt request is pending the scheduler hands over control to the sequencer.

The sequencer fetches the next instruction and places it in a register where it can be analysed by the translator. Subsequently the translator calls the microprogram appropriate to the instruction and the sequencer is again involved, since it is this unit which controls the flow of the microprogram.

Note Even though the internal structure of many computers is very different from the structure shown in figure 5.8, many systems have the characteristics of this arrangement when viewed externally. The same principle also applies for many time-sharing systems. A similar concept is found in the 'exchange unit' described by Berthelot, Duponchel and Vincon.* In this case the modules ALU, MS, etc., are considered to be

*Berthelot, Duponchel and Vincon, Final year project ENSI Mathématiques Appliquées et Informatique, Grenoble, June 1968.

'resources' which can for example be supplied by other computers. Systems viewed in this way open up many possibilities for linking several computers together, to form a network of computer resources.

6 Emulation

Emulation is the name given to the simulation of a real or hypothetical computer on the hardware of an existing machine. The aim of this simulation is to provide an environment for the execution of programs written for the emulated or *target* computer. In this context the computer on which the emulation is being done, is called the *host* machine.

Unlike a pure simulation, which is done entirely in software, emulation may involve modifications (usually extensions) to the host machine, not only in the software, but also in the hardware and microprogramming. The extent and type of these modifications is the subject of a complex compromise which hopefully optimises the performance–cost ratio. It should be pointed out in this introduction that emulation does not necessarily consist of providing the host with the instruction repertoire of the target machine, even if this appears to be the most direct approach.

We shall use the following plan in our discussion

(1) History of the problem; emulation as a by-product of microprogramming.
(2) Redefinition of the problem and relationship between translation and execution of a program.
(3) Implementation of emulators.
(4) Different types of emulators.
(5) Abstract machine emulators; relationship with interpretation.

6.1 History of the Problem

The first intensive use of microprogramming permitted IBM to design the 360 family of computers. The latter is characterised by

(a) the definition of an abstract machine (the term conceptual machine is also used);
(b) the development of this machine in various physical configurations, classified according to their individual performance.

It was discovered that with a given computer, or more precisely with a given set of resources, one could 'imitate' another machine and microprogramming quickly emerged as an ideal tool for this 'personalisation' of resources. For example, in parallel with IBM, two other companies began to sell 360-like machines: RCA (Spectra 70 series) and the Standard Computer Corporation. At first sight these companies appeared to be presenting machines in which the performance—cost ratio was achieved using hardware, software and microprogramming trade-offs that differed from those adopted by IBM. However, the search for flexibility and the successful emulation of new machines announced both by IBM and by other large computer companies, convinced the designers at RCA and SCC that they had in fact produced computers that could imitate other machines. IBM for their part, perfected 360 emulations of earlier IBM machines, especially the popular 1401, 7090–94 and 7040–44 models.

Another even more commercial aspect is the possibility of imitating a model of lesser performance marketed by another manufacturer. Such inter-manufacturer compatibility provides a fine opportunity for enticing away established customers, just when they are transferring to a larger model! (see reference 4, p. 310.)

In passing, we should note that the success of companies like RCA, SCC and also Interdata or Microsystems, which are successful specialists in the imitation of machines, is in part due to the fact that machines increasingly resemble one another, both in their structure and in their instruction repertoires.

The logical sequel to the success of imitating existing machines was to try to imitate hypothetical machines and even target computers having a high-level machine language. Examples of this approach include target computers with machine languages such as EULER (Wirth and Weber, 1965), APL (Hassit, Abrams, et al.), PL/I, Snobol, Algol, etc.

Another tempting direction has been to design a very flexible machine, on which to support a wide range of emulators. Such machines are often called universal emulators.

6.2 Comparison of Translation and Execution*

For greater clarity, let us consider an emulator as a simulation program for a target machine to be run on a suitably modified host computer. The main task for an emulator is therefore to accept as input a program in target-machine language and to provide the same output result as would have been obtained had the input program been run on the target machine. Seen thus, the program in target-machine language is input to the host-machine supervisor, which uses the emulator rather like a procedure.

*In this introductory section and in certain parts of sections 6.3.3 and 6.4.1, the author acknowledges his debt to the authoritative contributions made in this area by Stuart G. Tucker (see reference 15).

The emulator therefore has two functions: to translate the target-machine language into host-language, and to organise its execution. Because of pronounced resemblances between an emulator and the actual possession of the corresponding target machine, the two functions of translation and execution are very closely interleaved and should be clearly differentiated.

6.2.1 Translation

The translation process takes as input a program written in one language and generates an output in the form of a program in a second language which performs the same processing tasks. Well-known examples include

(a) a compiler generating a program in machine language from a program written in a high-level user language;

(b) an assembler of programs written in assembly language;

(c) a microprogram assembler written in symbolic form which supplies the binary content of the control memory as an output.

All these input languages have been conceived with a view to their translation into an executable language. This can be seen by noting that, in addition to directly executable statements which have a translation close to a one-to-one mapping, these languages also contain statements which provide additional information to assist the translation program (for example, EQUIVALENCE or DIMENSION statements in Fortran).

6.2.2 Execution

The execution process has an input in the form of a program expressed in executable language, together with an initial machine state. The execution procedure obeys the program instructions, modifies the machine state, and outputs results, as indicated by the instructions. Examples of execution procedures include

(a) a CII 10070 executing from the code in 10070 machine language;

(b) a simulator, running on a 10070, executing MITRA 15 code;

(c) an APL machine executing APL statements;

(d) a 7090 emulator running on a 360-65;

(e) an I/O channel executing the peripheral transfers dictated by a channel program.

There is therefore an executing machine and a machine state, or more generally, an execution process and a conceptual machine state.

Moreover, in the case of 'well-behaved' computer architectures, a given instruction or sequence of instructions will lead to a final machine state which is solely a function of the initial state, the machine architecture and the instructions being executed.

6.2.3 Comparison between Translator and Simulator

The translator exists simply to translate the target-language program into the host-machine language. Execution may or may not follow this translation and it therefore proves difficult to translate certain target instructions whey they are modified or replaced at the time of execution. (This translation problem almost requires an analysis of the programmer's motivation in choosing his instructions.)

On the other hand, in a simulator each instruction is interpreted and executed in sequence while a representation of the status of the target machine is kept in the host computer. With each target instruction the stored status information is updated, with the result that the difficulties in translation mentioned above are no longer encountered.

However, it should be noted that simulation is accompanied by an inherent loss in performance when compared with a translator. In a translator, once the translation is complete, the execution may proceed without further intervention, whereas with a simulator, interpretation is required during the execution of an instruction. Later we shall see another disadvantage of translation in the case of the replacement by emulation of a computer integrated with a complex computer network.

6.2.4 Comparison between a Simulator and an Emulator

According to our definition, a simulator is an emulator realised entirely by software. Simulation on a target machine presupposes

(a) A simulation of the target machine by representing its internal states and the processes which control the change of state, for example, state initialisation, recognition and modification.

(b) A simulation of the operations that are carried out with the orders contained in the instructions.

A simulator is implemented entirely in software, and is therefore based on a conceptual host machine (for example, a 360, without specifying which model).

In contrast, an emulator is founded on a particular host computer (for example, the 360-30) and where possible it will exploit the hardware resources of the host machine. For example, through modifications to the control unit (by embedding emulator routines within the control store) the emulator can have access to and therefore use of, the registers or the conditions bistables of the host computer; this brings a possible gain in performance with the attendant disadvantage that the emulator is peculiar to the host and cannot be transferred to a different computer. If necessary the hardware of the host machine can be modified in order to improve the emulator.

6.3 Implementation of Emulators

Three techniques are used, to provide the facilities necessary for emulation: programmed routines; microprogrammed routines; and hardware additions to the host machine.

6.3.1 Programmed Routines

There is little that can be said about programmed routines; they are pieces of software written for the conceptual host machine. However, there must be at least one special instruction enabling a programmed routine to communicate directly with microprogrammed routines, otherwise the slowness of processes, such as returning to a supervisor, would destroy the speed advantages of using a microprogram. An existing instruction can be used, provided that the corresponding microprogram is modified; for example, see the use of 'Diagnose' on certain IBM 360 machines.

6.3.2 Microprogrammed Routines

It will be appreciated that there are two categories of microprogrammed routine

(a) Those which are added to the host machine to simplify writing the emulation software or improve the simulator's performance. Routines of this sort frequently result in an increased instruction repertoire of the host machine.

(b) The second category concerns microprogramming of certain operations needed in the emulator. An example is provided by the subroutines corresponding to the simulation of target instructions, a technique which amounts to microprogramming target instructions directly on the host computer.

Both the above types of routine would be called in the same way by the emulation software. However, there is one small difference — those routines added to the conceptual host machine to extend its instruction repertoire can also be used in the assemblers, compilers, etc., of the host machine.

Having established the main types of routine, we shall now focus our attention on the workings of the microprogrammed part of an emulator. Here we shall assume a low-level target language using the simple instruction format of an operation code plus operand address.

It should be noted in passing that the microprogrammed routines, in so far as they are an extension of the control microprograms of the host machine, cost little when compared with the hardware changes that would be necessary in a host machine with wired control. (See chapter 4, section 4.1.)

6.3.3 Structure of an Emulator

For each target instruction the operation organised by the control unit of the target machine must be simulated. Figure 6.1 shows the flowchart of such a process. (Note that the loop should be broken at some point to check for interrupt requests.)

Viewed as an improved simulator, the emulator is an execution mechanism of the above operation, written on the host machine. It will therefore involve routines to perform operations such as

(a) address conversion and/or calculation;
(b) extraction of instructions from store;
(c) updating the target instruction counter;
(d) accessing operands;
(e) floating-point normalisation;
(f) field delimitation;
(g) simulating execution of various target instructions.

The first three routines correspond closely to the fetch phase of the flowchart in figure 6.1 and these routines are needed for each target instruction. Here we have a set of three routines which could usefully

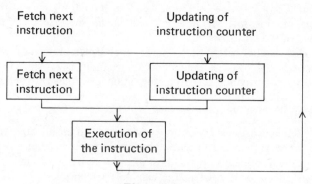

Figure 6.1

be replaced by a microprogram (or even a piece of hardware). Such an arrangement is generally considered to be an extension of the host's instruction repertoire and, like other instructions, they are given a mnemonic name. The new instruction suggested above is often called a DIL, for 'Do Interpretive Loop'. Examples of the functions performed by DIL are

(1) access the simulated instruction counter;
(2) after address conversion use the instruction counter as a pointer to the host memory cell containing the target instruction to be executed;
(3) fetch this instruction;
(4) update the simulated instruction counter (if a target word represents several host words this updating may involve rather more than simple incrementation);
(5) carry out any necessary indexing;
(6) fetch the operand(s);
(7) for each target instruction establish the starting address of the corresponding simulating routine, using the target Op code.

Among the above execution routines, the most frequently used will probably be microprogrammed. Another instruction which is often added is a quite general 'Branch if', which tests a target machine 'condition'. If the condition is satisfied the target instruction counter is loaded with the branch address and a DIL is used to emulate the branch. Conversely when the branch condition is not satisfied the emulator goes directly to the DIL.

As already indicated, DIL will use the target Op code, to determine the start address of each execution routine. Furthermore, DIL will address both the main and control memories. So far as accessing main store is concerned, even if it is more usual to use a table look-up, there is considerable advantage in establishing a simple arithmetic rule relating the start address of the execution routine to the target Op code. In applying such a rule, the DIL directly activates the execution routines and the latter are terminated either by the DIL instruction, if they programmed, or by a return to the DIL 'microprogram' if they are microprogrammed.

The gain in speed provided by microprogramming is explained by the absence of a fetch phase and the lower level (and therefore more flexible) forms of control.

Note We have just mentioned an instruction added to the repertoire of the host machine. It is not difficult to give it a mnemonic name (DIL, for example). However it is vital that the new instruction be given a binary operation code, and thus we assume that there are free Op codes available. In addition there must be sufficient space in the microprogram store to take these new routines.

6.3.4 Simulation of the Target Machine on the Host Computer

In essence this process involves simulating the addressable resources of target-machine language and the links between these resources (registers, main store, specialised processors, I/O channels, etc.) on the host machine.

The target main store will be simulated on the host memory (which can be a conceptual machine provided with a 'virtual memory', using both backing store as well as main memory). Registers of the target machine will be simulated by the fastest possible store locations in the hierarchy of host storage and the links between the target processes will be made, where possible, by the host-machine highways. The aim is therefore to map the target resources onto the most appropriate host resources and the more similar the host and target machines, the better the performance of the emulator.

The mapping problem is characterised by figure 6.2. Here the object is to simulate the box R and its interfacing connections L, using the host resource RR. The solution is to interpose other boxes between RR and the connections L in such a way as to give to RR the outward appearance of R.

Figure 6.2

Let us now consider a subset of the target machine (figure 6.3) made up of two target resources TR1 and TR2, connected by the target link TL.

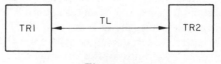

Figure 6.3

In figure 6.4 the corresponding host resources HR1 and HR2 with link HL are allocated (the resources can be real or virtual). Now it only

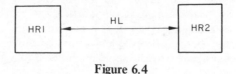

Figure 6.4

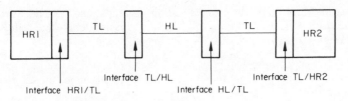

Figure 6.5

remains to supplement figure 6.4 with the appropriate interfaces, (figure 6.5) to obtain a device having no conceptual difference from that of figure 6.3.

The emulation largely consists of organising the various interfaces and necessary virtual resources. This organisation can be obtained by

(a) Software, in which only the resources of the conceptual host machine are usuable.

(b) Microprograms, whereby all resources, addressable from the host control store, can be used.

(c) Hardware, either by establishing the interface in hardware or by modifying the host resources (for example, by increasing the width of highway HL, or modifying the ALU to account for different operand coding, etc.) in order to simplify the interface design.

It is also possible to add supplementary hardware resources which can then be used by the microprogramming and hardware approaches. In practice in a microprogrammed host machine, the solution adopted is generally a compromise combination of all three techniques.

Functions often performed in the interfaces include series-to-parallel transformations, format generation, packing and unpacking, code translation, etc.

Conversion Problems We have just described the emulation of target resources and the operations dictated by the instructions, but we have not yet considered the problems of data representation.

Even assuming the target and host machines have the same length words, a boolean vector stored in a target memory cell has a significance which is not necessarily the same as a boolean vector in the host machine. The significance moreover, depends on the conventions involved. If the stored vector represents a number, the type of number needs to be considered; for example, integer or floating point. (Note in passing that certain instruction repertoires make no assumptions concerning the position of the binary/decimal point.) Alternatively this vector might represent a number in 2's complement form in one machine, and sign & (absolute value) convention in the other; similarly there may be differences due to decimal and binary representations. The necessary code translation or 'conversion' logically takes place in the interface, but its exact location depends on the emulator in question. Before pursuing this point in more detail the following examples of code conversion should be mentioned

(a) binary addressing, in a host memory with decimal addressing;

(b) decimal numbers in a 6-bit code on one machine, and 8-bit code on the other;

(c) processing of decimal operands (target) in a binary operator (host), etc.

Let us return to the problem of code conversion by examining an example. We shall consider the emulation of part of the target machine involving memory and ALU, and the operation involved will be the addition of two operands stored in the memory. This arrangement is shown diagrammatically in figures 6.6 and 6.7. (Note in figure 6.6 that it is unnecessary to distinguish between target link TL and host link HL.) Target memory TM contains decimal numbers and T ALU processes decimal operands, in decimal (see figure 6.7).

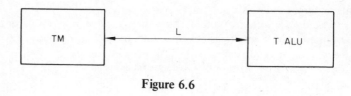

Figure 6.6

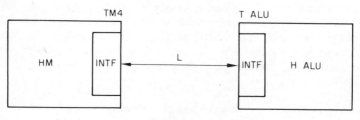

Figure 6.7

Considering this part of the target simulation there is a choice between several approaches, of which two are given below.

(1) In HM the numbers are stored in decimal, and the same representation is assumed on L. However the host arithmetic unit H ALU operates in binary and the code translation takes place at the L/H–ALU interface.

(2) Here the same hypotheses apply except that the H ALU is modified (for example, by inhibiting or forcing certain carry bits) in order to make it perform as a decimal adder. In this case therefore there is no conversion in the interface of the host ALU.

It is important to find a conceptual framework for the second approach given above, where there is no conversion in the interface transferring the data. A conceptual framework is important for it permits a methodical approach to more complicated cases. Here for example it can be considered that we have modified the interface between the control unit and the ALU of the host computer. The ALU interprets the addition order knowing that the emulation of a decimal machine requires a decimal addition. Interpretation is effected at the level of the ALU, or in the control unit. In fact interpretation can be seen as an interface between control unit and ALU, where it is commands rather than data which undergo conversion. The overall objective is to establish coherence between the command language used to control the ALU and the language used to represent operands of, or results generated by, the ALU.

In the second of the above cases it can be considered that the execution routine of the target addition (in decimal) uses a virtual procedure which in turn uses the real ALU. This contrasts with the first case where the ALU is addressed directly and has an interpreter in the form of an interface.

While discussing conversion problems, it should be pointed out that the conversion itself should be 'well behaved'. It is necessary to have a mapping f of the set of decimal operands onto the corresponding set of binary operands. Also if an operation T in the target machine is replaced by an operation H in the host machine, then H and f are well selected, if f is a structure isomorphism, such that

$$\forall_{x,y} \quad xTy = f^{-1}(f(x)Hf(y))$$

This mapping is illustrated in figure 6.8; however one aspect of the translation not emphasised in the diagram is that it is important to establish a one-to-one relation between target and host-machine states, before and after operations T and H.

When considering the emulation of a decimal machine on a binary host, the question arises of whether, at a particular interface, it is really

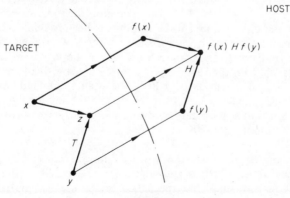

Figure 6.8

necessary to transfer between decimal and binary representations. After all, we know the programs are originally written in decimal and the translation, for binary machines, takes place in the I/O unit. The overall problem is one of the emulation of a decimal conceptual machine used by a programmer on a real binary machine. The assembler moreover carries out a part of the emulation in the form of the translation of the mnemonic codes into machine code, and the conversion of 'literal' operands into binary. However, the preceding pages would lead one to believe that the proper method would be to simulate the *decimal* instructions. In practice the approach adopted when designing an emulator is governed by the prevailing systems requirements and constraints. This aspect will be considered in the following sections which describe four different types of emulation.

6.4 Different Types of Emulator

We shall consider the following types of emulator: specialised emulators; current commercial emulators; universal emulators; and interpretive machines, whose role transcends that of simple emulators since they allow conceptual machines to be implemented in high-level symbolic language.

6.4.1 Specialised Emulators

Specialised emulators were historically the first emulators to be used. They can be treated as an extension to a real (that is, not conceptual) host machine which allows the emulation of a particular (real) target machine. The components of such an extension are often assembled in a single hardware unit, which then constitutes an optional piece of equipment. These emulators are offered by manufacturers to provide software compatibility when a customer changes to a larger computer (see reference 4, pp. 309–10). The emulator thus allows programs written for the old computer to be run on the new machine and once the customer has rewritten his software for the new machine, he will return the emulator to the manufacturer. For example, the emulation of the IBM 1620 on the IBM 360-30 is made up of a simulator and a microprogrammed extension of a little less than 4000 words with no other hardware modification. In this example the microprogrammed extension constitutes a separate hardware unit which is easily attached or detached from the 360-30.

Emulation of Inputs and Outputs Although the emulation of input/output comes a little outside the realm of specialised emulators, it is described here since, like specialised emulators, the emulation of

I/O devices should be considered when changing to a new computer. When updating a computer installation, it must be established whether the peripheral equipment of the old machine is to be used with the new equipment. In a computer centre for example, when the machine is to be changed, the peripherals are generally changed as well. On the other hand, if a computer in a complex computer network is to be replaced, the previous connections must be preserved both logically as well as physically. For the present however, we shall assume that the peripherals are replaced and the new ones must emulate the old. Having made this assumption the magnetic tapes of the target machine – the old tapes – must be read and rewritten. Also assuming the tape translation is to be done on the new (host) machine, an I/O is initialised with the aid of instructions from the host machine and the interrupts generated by the tape peripheral are therefore returned to the host machine. While these interrupts will be serviced between host instructions, the transfer of information to the target machine will only occur between executions of target instructions.

Interrupt synchronisation can be organised using the DIL instruction. In the case of an I/O interrupt generation by a peripheral unit the host program which services the interrupt updates a status word (possibly a single bit) and hands back control to the emulator at that point where the latter was interrupted. It is therefore necessary to include a test in DIL to check this status word (*cf.* the interrupt check in the FETCH of the normal in-sequence instruction) with the possibility of branching to the target interrupt servicing routine.

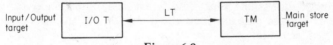

Figure 6.9

The problem of emulating peripheral transfers is shown by figure 6.9, in which the I/O units are assumed to have direct access to the main store. TM must be mapped onto a part of the host memory HM, and we will use the notation H*M to represent the image of TM in HM. Also as one might expect, the target I/O functions are emulated using the I/O host unit which is closest to the target requirements. If we now add the necessary conversion interfaces, we arrive at the functional diagram of figure 6.10.

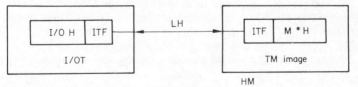

Figure 6.10

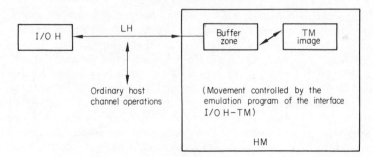

Figure 6.11

The location of the interfaces again presents a problem. If the host I/O channel is easily modifiable (for example, if the host is micro-programmed), the interface will be microprogrammed directly as shown figure 6.10. Conversely, if it is difficult to establish the interface at the level of the I/O channel, it must be done within the central memory. This requires a buffer zone, figure 6.11, filled or emptied via the host I/O channel. In such a case, a conversion program is used to fill or empty the image of the target store from the buffer zone.

Exchanges between I/O and buffer zones are done using normal host peripheral operations. They can therefore be done simultaneously with the operations in the central processor unit. On the other hand, movements between the buffer and the image zone cannot be so easily disengaged from the CPU. Figures 6.12a and b (see reference 15) illustrate this point using both input and output operations; in particular these diagrams show the overlap in I/O channel operations and CPU emulation.

Emulation of a Computer while Conserving its Environment   Let us take an example to illustrate this type of emulation (see reference 14). Towards the middle of 1970, the United States Air Force Space and Missile Organisation needed to update its satellite guidance system. The system included twelve interconnected CDC 160A computers, which were ten years old. Although the hardware was showing signs of weakness, the software, consisting of about one million instructions, formed a complete operational system, which was working in real time and had been patiently debugged over the life of the system.

It was decided therefore to keep the original software and replace the hardware with new equipment exhibiting the same hardware characteristics, but with the advantage of increased speed and reliability.

In short, it was necessary to preserve the acquired software reliability and improve the hardware reliability. It quickly appeared that the solution was to emulate the old 160A computers on a more

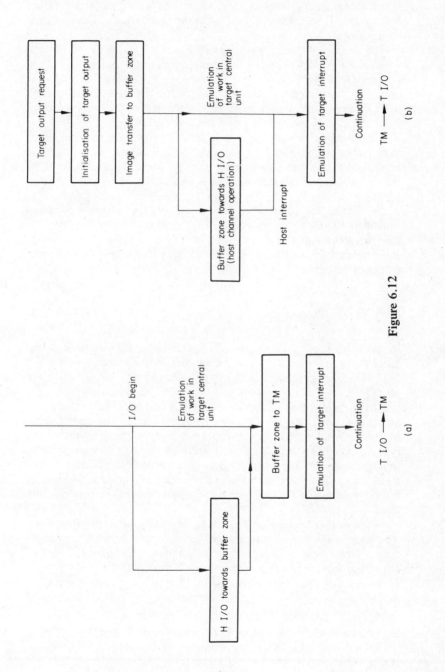

Figure 6.12

recent machine, and what is more, the emulation should represent the
160A just as it was, without yielding to the temptation of incorporating
improvements.

The host computer was chosen from the category of general
commercial emulators that will be discussed in the following section.
Despite the original emulation philosophy, the emulated 160A was
eventually improved: its OP code extended (by adding instructions
using binary configurations not previously used) and two bootstraps
were microprogrammed in the read-only control store.

This example also allows us to highlight a particular problem which
arises when the emulated computer is to work in real time. Real time
requirements are generally translated by the specification of a response
time, the value of which must fall between maximum and minimum
limits.

For example, suppose a subroutine of the original computer
simulated a clock by depending on the duration (assumed uniform) of
the instructions in a loop. In such a case it is necessary to re-examine
the emulated subroutine loop to check that the timing falls between
necessary limits.

6.4.2 Current General Commercial Emulators

In chapter 5 we referred to the general-purpose emulator as an
'amorphous' machine. As already described their hardware consists of a
collection of registers, memory stacks, buses, etc., all of which are
controlled by microprogram. Usually the various functions and
resources are designed using a quantum of 4 or 8 bits. Furthermore, the
instruction repertoire itself is not fixed and can be changed through
microprogramming, the microinstructions being of the mini-instruction
type to simplify their use. Such facilities allow the manufacturer to
supply assemblers and microprogram simulators to his customers and
there is also the possibility of manufacturing supporting equipment —
for example, hardware to organise the initial 'writing' of the read-only
store.

We have mentioned that the hardware takes the form of an easily
controlled collection of resources and an example should illustrate this
point. Many machines have instruction repertoires based on 1, 2, 4, 8 or
16 accumulators. Hence an emulator will probably have one or two
16-word scratch-pad memories of 8 or 16 bits with which to represent
accumulators.

Computers typical of this class of machine are

(a) M.E.T.A. 4 from Scientific Data Corporation, San Diego, U.S.A.
(b) IC 5000 from Standard Computer Corporation, Santa Anna,
U.S.A.
(c) Multi-8 and -20 from Intertechnique, France.

The success of these emulators is equally interesting from the point of view of the standardisation of hardware components. For example, the MITRA 15 computer from C.I.I. had two processing units: one arithmetic and logic unit and one exchange handling unit. Actually these two units are identical and only the microprograms that control them are different. Amorphous machines basically follow the same idea, but at a lower level.

6.4.3 Universal Study Emulators

Commercial machines designed specifically for emulation generally have similar machine structures. Also as one might expect, they do not perform as well as a more directly designed computer. Nevertheless this loss in performance is acceptable, provided it is suitably compensated in other areas (cost, development time, etc.).

During the development of a new machine, it is tempting for a large manufacturer to use a special computer which behaves like an easily modifiable prototype, that is, a machine whose configuration is easily changed. It follows that it is necessary to adopt some of the techniques used for general-purpose commercial emulators: some scratch-pads to emulate easily addressable registers (the ICL-E1 has 256 words), main stores in 8-bit bytes, several buses, etc. Since each of the resources becomes a host for a target resource, it is desirable to arrange for the emulation interface to be placed at the input/output of each physical host resource. These interfaces must be easily modifiable and ideally they should be dynamically microprogrammed.

So far as the main store is concerned, if it is possible to separate program and data stores, it becomes possible to consider data and program look-ahead mechanisms. It is equally desirable to be able to organise the main store into long words with a field of the word acting as a descriptor.

Various arithmetic and logic operators are also required. It should be mentioned here that associative memories can be used as universal operators, by using a table look-up approach and storing the table in the associative memory. For small tables, the cost does not present a problem and in many cases, the size of the table can be reduced if an operator is available such that there is an isomorphism of the type mentioned towards the end of the section 6.3. The table is searched for the isomorphic representation of each operand and, after these have been processed by the appropriate operator, the result is reconverted using the table.

One final and very important aspect of 'study emulators' is the provision for the quantitative assessment of the target machine's performance. Apart from 'benchmark' job mixes which can be run on any machine, the study emulator itself should have built-in hardware monitoring facilities.

6.5 Interpretive Machines

Interpretive machines can be defined as those in which the control unit interprets a high-level machine language, resembling the established user programming languages.

The interpretation is complicated by the fact that the position of a bit or character in an instruction is not necessarily sufficient to define its meaning. We should remember that in an instruction of fixed format, the position of a bit in the instruction word completely defines its meaning. (This is reflected in the way that the definition of the instruction formats constitutes part of the physical description of the computer.) In an interpretive machine, format definition should form part of the syntax rules of the control unit. It follows that, when reading a string of characters, this type of control unit seeks to delimit the executable units of the string. From this point of view, string languages (like APL) are more practical than block languages (such as Algol, PL/1, etc.).

A more radical means of creating a high-level input language machine M is to emulate machine M on a more conventional machine H (H representing host or hardware). An output interface M is arranged on machine H. If the language of M is very high level, while that of H is a traditional machine language it is desirable to establish a sequence of interfaces: M, ... M3, M2, M1, whose languages increasingly resemble that of H. This can be represented by a diagram as shown in figure 6.13.

The hierarchy of interfaces are referred to as 'levels of machines' or 'nested machines'. Since H is a conventional machine, the different intermediary machines M1, M2, M3, ... are achieved by software alone. Simulating machine Mi means programming on Mi-1 and it is wise when creating Mi to use only the resources of Mi-1. In other words, the direct use of the resources of Mi-2, Mi-3, ... is consciously avoided.

Let us suppose that we want to realise an interpretive machine (that is, a machine accepting a control language similar to high-level programming languages) by establishing a system of nested machines as described above. The temptation will be to provide H with hardware additions that improve the performance of M. We shall consider this point in more detail.

We shall assume that M includes an instruction of type $T(a,b,c)$. Suppose, that as an improvement, it is proposed that an instruction $T(x,y,z)$ is added to H. The problem is one of retaining, from level to level, the improvement in performance brought about by the inclusion of $T(x,y,z)$ in H. Certainly interpretation is simplified since T is easily available in each machine. On the other hand, in each machine the operands are designated by symbolic names to which addresses in the more internal machine must correspond. This mechanism, which occurs between adjacent levels, is carried out in an interpretive mode for each operation.

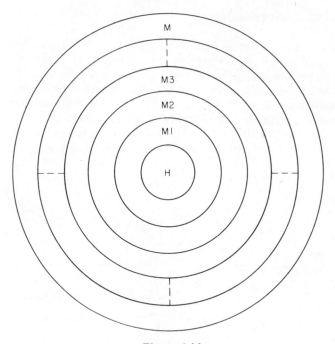

Figure 6.13

If T is simple (a p or v on signal, for example*) the improvement in performance by using T directly rather than simulating it is negligible compared with the mappings necessary in subsequent addresses. In fact in some circumstances, using T directly can prove a significant disadvantage. The same argument applies to p. If p is not used, it will be easy to decrement within one of the algorithms between adjacent levels and at the level of H this will become a complete instruction.

The above is not generally true when using a compiler where (in contrast to the interpretive approach) the mappings are done during the compilation process. Here the improvement anticipated by realising T in hardware is made up without loss.

We therefore conclude that when operating in interpretive mode, the addition of extra hardware is not usually justified except for address mapping. For operations involving pure processing, it is better to seek very general-purpose hardware.

We shall not consider interpretive machines any further for they seem to lie outside the framework of this book. However, one cannot fail to notice the utility of the associative processes, dynamic microprogramming, etc., for implementing these machines.

*Using Dikjstra's notation.

6.6 Performance of Emulators

Emulator performance is treated in the articles by Tucker (reference 20), May, Iliffe and Rackocsi (reference 15) and in a workshop on microprogramming (reference 14). Also Iliffe (reference 19) has assembled and authoritatively commented on much of the information contained in the above references. Although we shall not pursue this topic any further here, it is hoped that the mechanisms of emulation have been sufficiently described in this chapter to allow an appreciation of where the performance trade-offs occur.

Appendix A
Minimisation of Microprograms

A.1 Wired or Programmed Realisation of an Algorithm

An algorithm is a systematic and unambiguous procedure for processing data. We know that an algorithm can be executed using a stored-program computer, but we can also envisage a unit which will perform the same processing operations and thus generate the same result. The output may take the form of a sequence of results spaced out in time, a situation which assumes that the input data are also spaced in time. Examples of such units are multipliers, dividers, counters, etc.

We have also seen how the command and execution circuits of a computer can be simplified by microprogramming, that is, storing the micro-algorithms in a command store. We shall now consider the relationship between the two points of view in more detail.

A.2 Synchronous Finite-state Automata (Synchronous Finite-state Machines)

A machine can be defined in terms of the following 4-tuple

$\underset{\sim}{Q}, \underset{\sim}{E}, f, H$

where $\underset{\sim}{Q}$ is a set of values taken by a variable Q, called the state variable of the machine;

$\underset{\sim}{E}$ is a set of values taken by a variable E, called the input (or command) variable of the machine;

Q and E are variables synchronised by the same clock signal H;

f is a 'next state' function of the form

$$Q_{t+1} = f(Q_t, E_t)$$

Two extra parameters $\{\underset{\sim}{S}, g\}$ are often added to the above list, where $\underset{\sim}{S}$ is the set of values of a variable S called the output variable, (also synchronised by H) and g is an output function of the form

$$S_t = g(Q_t, E_t)$$

or

$$S_{t+1} = g(Q_t, E_t)$$

the 6-tuple $\{Q, E, S, f, g, H\}$ then represents a finite-state machine with its output function.

A.2.1 Synchronous Automata in Computers

The sets Q, E and S are finite. Q possesses an element Q^0, called the 'initial state', such that for every value Q^i of Q there is a sequence

$$Q^i+1, \ldots Q^{i+j}, \ldots Q^{i+n+1} = Q^0$$

and a sequence

$$E^{i+1}, \ldots E^{i+j}, \ldots E^{i+n}$$

such that

$$Q^{i+j+1} = f(Q^{i+j}, E^{i+j}), \quad j \epsilon \{0, 1, \ldots n\}$$

A.2.2 State Table of a Finite-state Machine

The functions f and g are often described by means of two adjacent tables as in table A.1.

Table A.1

Q_t	Q_{t+1}					S_t or S_{t+1}				
E_t	E^0	E^1	E^2	$\ldots$	E^p	E^0	E^1	E^2	$\ldots$	E^p
Q^0	Q^{00}	Q^{01}	Q^{02}		Q^{0p}	S^{00}	S^{01}	S^{02}		S^{0p}
Q^1	Q^{10}	Q^{11}	Q^{12}		Q^{1p}	S^{10}	S^{11}	S^{12}		S^{1p}
.	.	.	.		.	.	.	.		.
.	.	.	.		.	.	.	.		.

A.2.3 Definition in the Form of a Microprogram

Q can be organised to form the set of rows of a microprogram in such a way that table A.1 becomes

$$Q^0 - \text{if } E = E^0 \text{ make } S = S^{00} \text{ and go to } Q^{00} \text{ if not}$$
$$Q^0 - \text{if } E = E^1 \text{ make } S = S^{01} \text{ and go to } Q^{01} \text{ if not}$$

.
.
.

Q^0 – if $E = E^p$ make $S = S^{0p}$ and go to Q^{0p}

Q^1 – if $E = E^0$ make S^{10} and go to Q^{10} if not

Q^2 – if $E = E^0$ make $S = S^{20}$ and go to Q^{20} if not

.
.
.

If the rows Q^i of the program thus defined, are felt to be too long, they can be broken down as shown below for row Q^0 of the above program

Q^0 – 0 if $E = E^0$ make $S = S^{00}$ and go to Q^{00} if not go to Q^0 – 1

Q^0 – 1 if $E = E^1$ make $S = S^{01}$ and go to Q^{01} if not go to Q^0 – 2

Q^0 – 2 if $E = E^2$ make $S = S^{02}$ and go to Q^{02} if not go to Q^0 – 3

.
.
.

Q^0 – p if $E = E_p$ make $S = S^{0p}$ and go to Q^{0p}

A.2.4 Wired or Programmed Realisation

The aim of a finite-state machine is to obtain an output sequence from the corresponding sequence of the input variable. The state variable is used to take account of the state of the procedure.

We have seen in chapter 6 that Q, E and S can take the form of electric signals and the finite-state machine was then realised in the form of a synchronised sequential circuit with the aid of logic circuits. Thus the state table definition is well suited to the design of computers.

In a computer the sequential machine can be realised in the form of a stored program rather than using a specially designed sequential circuit. Therefore, we shall draw an analogy between a program (strictly a microprogram) and a finite-state machine.

A.2.5 Representing a Microprogram as a Moore Machine

We shall consider a series of memory locations containing a micro-algorithm and the associated address register (figure A.1). The latter points to the address of the instruction to be decoded and then executed.

This can be considered as a Moore machine, in other words a machine with an output function of the $S_{t+1} = g(Q_t, E_t)$. The state at time t is characterised by the state of the memory word read at time t;

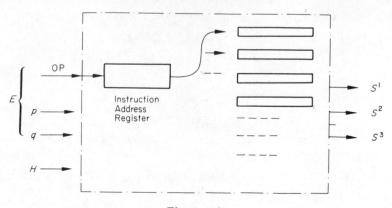

Figure A.1

the clock input is H; the outputs of the system are the signals s^1, s^2, s^3, ... which are obtained by the decoding of the instruction. These are the signals which in time $(t + 1)$ will control elementary operations such as shifting a register, setting a bit in memory, transferring a unit of information from one register to another, incrementing the contents of a register, etc. (It is assumed that there is no output register after the command store.)

Sometimes the output signal does not control an operator — a good example is a conditional switch in the flow of the microprogram. Such an output s is found in states 3 and 4 of the example below.

The inputs are

(a) an input corresponding to the microprogram operation which serves to determine the cleared condition, that is, the first store location to be read;

(b) variables p, q, ... which are the criteria for branching in the microprogram. For example $q = 1$ will indicate that the accumulator is negative and $p = 1$ will indicate that a certain counter is equal to zero, etc.

The micro-algorithm can then be regarded as a Moore machine whose states are the rows of the algorithm. As an example we shall take the classic non-restoring devision algorithm using repeated subtraction (or adding) and shifting.

Dividend = accumulator; Divisor = $R1$; Quotient = $R2$

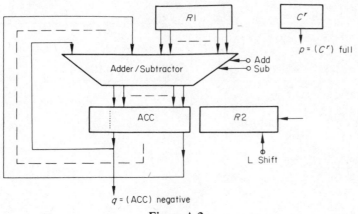

Figure A.2

1.	Shift ACC left	(s^1)
2.	Put ACC = ACC $-$ R1	(s^2)
3.	If counter full $(p = 1)$ go to 12	(a)
	If not go to 4	
4.	If ACC negative $(q = 1)$ go to 9	(a)
	If not go to 5	
5.	Put rightmost bit of $R2 = 1$	(s^3)
6.	Shift $R2$ left and put $C^r = C^r + 1$	(s^4)
7.	Shift ACC left	(s^1)
8.	Put ACC = ACC + $R1$ and go to 3	(s^2)
9.	Shift $R2$ left and put $C^r = C^r + 1$	(s^4)
10.	Shift ACC left	(s^1)
11.	Put ACC = ACC + $R1$ and go to 3	(s^5)
12.	END	

Let us put the algorithm in the form of a table (table A.2). In the 'output' column only the signal of value 1 is indicated.

State 12 has no specified following states and generally this will represent a waiting condition. If however this was the only stored algorithm the state table would probably indicate a return to the cleared condition preceding state 1.

A.2.6 First Minimisation Step

The formal minimisation methods of the Moore automata can be applied to the above machine. For example states 1 and 7, and 2 and 8 are equivalent, resulting in the new table A.3.

Table A.2

Q_t	Q_{t+1} Input $(pq)_t$:				Output
	00	01	10	11	
1	2	2	2	2	s^1
2	3	3	3	3	s^2
3	4	4	12	12	
4	5	9	5	9	
5	6	6	6	6	s^3
6	7	7	7	7	s^4
7	8	8	8	8	s^1
8	3	3	3	3	s^2
9	10	10	10	10	s^4
10	11	11	11	11	s^1
11	3	3	3	3	s^5
12	–	–	–	–	u

Table A.3

Present state	Next state Input pq :				Output
	00	01	10	11	
1	2	2	2	2	s^1
2	3	3	3	3	s^2
3	4	4	10	10	
4	5	7	6	7	
5	6	6	6	6	s^3
6	1	1	1	1	s^4
7	8	8	8	8	s^4
8	9	9	9	9	s^1
9	3	3	3	3	s^5
10	–	–	–	–	u

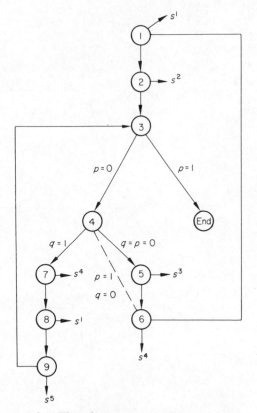

Figure A.3 Flowchart corresponding to table A.2

It is interesting to establish the flowcharts (figures A.3 and A.4) corresponding to the two equivalent automata (the use of flowcharts being equally applicable to state tables or programs written line-by-line).

It is apparent, from the first flowchart, that states 7 and 8 are of no use since from state 6, the sequence of outputs is s^1, s^2 finishing at state 3, and that the same result is obtained by jumping directly from state 6 to state 1 as in the second flowchart (figure A.4).

Thus by employing formal minimisation methods we have been able to simplify the flowchart. However, by exploiting certain properties of the microprograms themselves, we can go one step further.

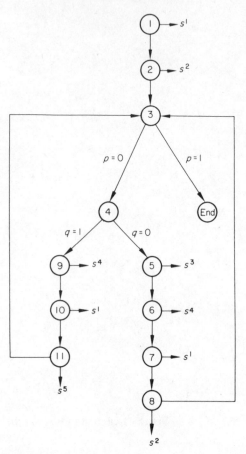

Figure A.4   Flowchart corresponding to table A.3

A.2.7 Second Minimisation Step

As already described a microprogram involves transitions that are not accompanied by output signals (that is, do not involve signals for the execution networks) and as a consequence the microprogram test does not constitute a step in time. The result of the test is produced in the form of a logical signal (for example, the sign bit of a register) and, using suitable switching logic, the algorithm follows one path rather than another.

This microprogram behaviour allows minimisations that did not occur in the first step. Such is the case with 'states' 3 and 4 which can then be combined with state 2. The resultant table is shown in table A.4 and the corresponding flow diagram is given in figure A.5. It appears that the second minimisation step (which involves a careful

Table A.4

Q_t	Q_{t+1} Input $(pq)_t$				Output
	00	01	10	11	
1	2	2	2	2	s^1
2	3	5	8	8	s^2
3	4	4	4	4	s^3
4	1	1	1	1	s^4
5	6	6	6	6	s^4
6	7	7	7	7	s^1
7	3	5	8	8	s^5
8	—	—	—	—	

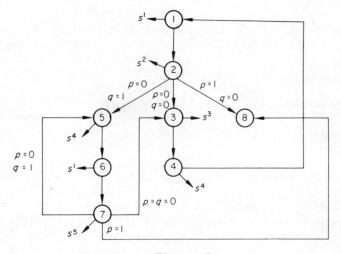

Figure A.5

scrutiny of the tests) can be applied more easily to the flowchart than
to the table.

A.2.8 Third Minimisation Step

If the microprograms are stored in the read-only memories such that
the operation is analogous to a Mealy machine (output function of the
form $S_t = g(E_t, Q_t)$) the number of states can again be reduced by
formal methods.

Appendix B
Controlled Graphs and Instructions

In chapter 3 it was shown that designing a microinstruction was equivalent to selecting a subgraph of the graph symbolising the computer. Here we shall develop this approach by concerning ourselves with the determination of the result of an instruction and hence the result of a succession of instructions.

B.1 Instruction

An instruction has been defined in the main text as a mapping of the set of edges of the controlled graph G of a computer on to a reduced graph G_p. The connectivity matrix of the partial graph G_p is then a partial matrix of the connectivity matrix M associated with the graph G itself.

An instruction can be defined equivalently as a partial matrix P of the matrix M. It is this aspect that will be chiefly used in the following discussion. (Figure B.1 provides an example.)

B.2 Controlled Graph

As described in chapter 3 we call a directed graph G, for which a non-empty set of instructions has been defined, a controlled graph.

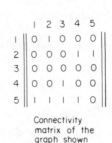

	1	2	3	4	5
1	0	1	0	0	0
2	0	0	0	1	1
3	0	0	0	0	0
4	0	0	1	0	0
5	1	1	1	1	0

Connectivity matrix of the graph shown

0	1	0	0	0
0	0	0	0	1
0	0	0	0	0
0	0	0	0	0
0	0	1	0	0

Instruction
1 ← 2 → 3 ← 5 for the same graph

Figure B.1

B.3 Algebra of Instructions Definable on a Controlled Graph

For the boolean operations of intersection ($\cdot$) and summation (+) term-by-term (or bit-by-bit) of the connectivity matrices, the instructions definable on a directed graph G, form a boolean algebra. The unit element or maximum instruction is the connection matrix M of the graph itself. The null instruction is the partial matrix Z whose terms are all zero. The order relation between submatrices (or instructions) is naturally given by

$$T \geqslant S \Leftrightarrow T + S = T$$

The dimension of the algebra is the number n of edges of the graph since this is the number of 1s in the matrix M.

Complement of an instruction T (denoted T')

We denote the complement of an instruction T as T', where

$$T' = M \oplus T$$

in which $\oplus$ represents addition modulo 2 (exclusive OR) term-by-term (or bit-by-bit).

Bit complement of an Instruction T, denoted by $\bar{T}$
Generally, $T' \neq \bar{T}$

Product of two instructions
Let A and B be two instructions, $A = \| a_{ij} \|$, $B = \| b_{ii} \|$.

The product of these two instructions, taken in the order given is written as $A \times B$, and may be defined in terms of the matrix $C = \| c_{ij} \|$ as follows

$$C_{ij} = \sum_{k=1}^{n} a_{ik} \cdot b_{kj}$$

where Σ represents boolean summation (OR), and $a_{ik} \cdot b_{kj}$ denotes boolean intersection (AND).

It is known that this product is associative, that is

$$(A \times B) \times C = A \times (B \times C) = A \times B \times C$$

The nth power of a matrix T, $n \geqslant 1$, denoted by T^n may be defined as

$$T^n = T^{n-1} \times T, \quad n > 1, \quad T^1 = T$$

The transitive closure $\hat{T}$, of a matrix T

$$\hat{T} = T + T^2 + T^3 + \ldots T^n + T^{n+1} + \ldots$$

(this sum can become prematurely stabilised).

The transpose A_T of a matrix A
If $A = \| a_{ij} \|$ then $A_T = \| \alpha_{ij} \|$, where $\alpha_{ij} = a_{ji}$

We note that $(\bar{A})_T = (\overline{A_T})$ and will denote this simply by $\bar{A}_T$

Note on the product of instructions

If $C = A \times B$, that is $c_{ij} = \sum_{k=1}^{n} a_{ik} \cdot b_{kj}$

then $c_{ij} = 1 \Leftrightarrow \exists\, k$, such that $a_{ik} = b_{kj} = 1$

This means that there is an edge going from node i to node k, and similarly, an edge going from the node k to the node j. Therefore a directed path of length 2 exists, leading from i via k to j. It now follows that M^2 indicates paths of length 2 and more generally a term $m_{ij} = 1$ in M^n indicates that there is at least one path of length n between vertices i and j.

A product of instructions is not necessarily an instruction. In general, if

$$T = T_1 \times T_2 \times \ldots \times T_n$$

is an instruction, then for every directed path of length n, defined by this product, there is an edge joining its source to its termination.

Stable instruction
A stable instruction T has a partial graph with no cycle or loop; that is, the diagonal of $\hat{T}$ is null.

B.4 Matrix of Maximum Paths Defined by Instruction

This matrix, denoted by $T^\%$, gives the maximum (longest) non-cyclic paths defined by the instruction T. When two maximum paths have the same origin vertex and the same final vertex, they are not differentiated. This matrix is given by $\hat{T}$ in which the terms (ij) are cancelled such that $\exists\, k$, where (ki), or $(jk) = 1$. $T^\%$ can be defined as follows

$$T^\% = (\overline{U \times T})_T \cdot (\overline{T \times U})_T \cdot \hat{T}$$

Where U denotes the square matrix with all terms equal to 1, and whose dimension is determined by context.

$\hat{T}$ gives the non-closed paths of all the lengths (less than n).

$(U \times T)$ gives a column j only containing 1s. When the column j of T is non-null and a column of $U \times T$ is either null or full of 1s. A column j of $U \times T$ is null if and only if the column j is null in T.

$(U \times T)_T$ gives a row j full of 1s provided the column j of T is non-null.

To clarify what follows, we shall use C_j to describe column j, and R_j to describe row j.

In $(U \times T)$, $\left\{ \begin{array}{l} C_j = 1 \ldots 1 \Leftrightarrow C_j \neq 0 \ldots 0 \\ C_j = 0 \ldots 0 \Leftrightarrow C_j = 0 \ldots 0 \end{array} \right\}$ in T

$$\text{In } (U \times T)_T, \quad \begin{cases} R_j = 1 \ldots 1 \Leftrightarrow C_j \neq 0 \ldots 0 \\ R_j = 0 \ldots 0 \Leftrightarrow C_j = 0 \ldots 0 \end{cases} \text{ in } T$$

$$\text{In } \overline{(U \times T)}_T \quad \begin{cases} R_j = 0 \ldots 0 \Leftrightarrow C_j \neq 0 \ldots 0 \\ R_j = 1 \ldots 1 \Leftrightarrow C_j = 0 \ldots 0 \end{cases} \text{ in } T$$

Following this, $(\overline{U \times T})_T$ selects in $\hat{T}$ rows R_j such that no edge arrives in j, therefore j can be the origin of a maximum path.

$$\text{In } (T \times U), \quad \begin{cases} R_j = 1 \ldots 1 \Leftrightarrow R_j \neq 0 \ldots 0 \\ R_j = 0 \ldots 0 \Leftrightarrow R_j = 0 \ldots 0 \end{cases} \text{ in } T$$

$$\text{In } (T \times U)_T, \quad \begin{cases} C_j = 1 \ldots 1 \Leftrightarrow R_j \neq 0 \ldots 0 \\ C_j = 0 \ldots 0 \Leftrightarrow R_j = 0 \ldots 0 \end{cases} \text{ in } T$$

$$\text{In } \overline{(T \times U)}_T, \quad \begin{cases} C_j = 0 \ldots 0 \Leftrightarrow R_j \neq 0 \ldots 0 \\ C_j = 1 \ldots 1 \Leftrightarrow R_j = 0 \ldots 0 \end{cases} \text{ in } T$$

Subsequently $(\overline{T \times U})_T$ eliminates the vertices j in T which are non-terminal vertices of maximum paths ($R_j \neq 0 \ldots 0$, implies that it is possible to go from j towards another vertex, thus j is not the terminal vertext of a path).

Finally, a term $(i,j) = 1$ in $T^\%$ indicates that there is at least one path going from i to j; that no edge arrives at i; and that no edge leaves from j.

Note. Cycles are thus eliminated and this is not necessarily desirable. If one wishes to take account of these cycles, it is necessary to modify the above expression by adding (boolean union) a term of the form $T \times I = \hat{T} \cdot I$. Here I is the matrix, with only the diagonal terms equal to 1, the dimension again being fixed by content.

If T is the maximum instruction, that is $T = M$, the matrix associated with the graph, then $M^\%$ gives the maximum paths of the graph.

B.5 Physical Significance of an Instruction

A term $(i,j) = 1$ of an instruction indicates that a direct path (or edge) from i toward j is allowed. If $(i,j) = 0$, this means either that there is no direct path from i towards j, or that this path, if it exists, is forbidden.

A network provided with instructions can for example be a set of streets with traffic lights or a network of operators and electronic storage elements whose connections are controlled by AND gates, as is the case in a computer.

B.6 Result of an Instruction

This is a concept which assumes its full importance when successive instructions are considered. Let T be an instruction, then we shall denote T^R as its result. The expression of the result of two successive instructions is determined by the nature of the flow.

T^R defines where the flow starts and where it terminates. Thus there is the implicit hypothesis that the speeds in the various paths are such that at the beginning of the instruction, the flow leaves the departure vertices, and at the end of the instruction, the flow arrives at the arrival vertices. We shall consider the case in which the speed of the flow is small in relation to the duration of the instruction. For example, if the flow can only cross three successive edges in the course of an instruction it will be necessary to replace $\hat{T}$ by $T + T^2 + T^3$ in the formula giving $T^\%$. Also it may be necessary to add intermediary vertices to compensate for unequal transmission speeds. For an instruction considered in isolation, T^R is similar to $T^\%$. However, we shall see that in one case, that of a 'tagging flow', $T^R \neq T^\%$.

B.7 Various Types of Flow

Flows may be characterised by the discrete elements of information involved. Below we shall define three types of flow and establish for each type the expression giving the result of two successive instructions.

A Network with Transient Flow   Electronic pulse signals, are transient in the sense that they must be used at the moment in time that they exist.

A Network with Indestructible Flow   An example of indestructible flow is found in vehicles in a town whose circulation is controlled by traffic lights. For a given state of the traffic lights in the town (that is, for a certain instruction) a vehicle continues on its route provided it encounters green lights. When a vehicles comes across a red light, it stops and waits (without risk of disappearing!) until an instruction sets the light to green.

A Network with Tagging Flow   In this type of flow, the flow element 'marks' (leaves a copy of) its value at the vertices of the path that the instruction assigns it to follow. Thus, a subsequent instruction can test the value in any vertex of the path in question, provided of course that in the meantime, this vertex has not been changed to a new value.

Result of Two Successive Instructions   Like the result of a single instruction, the result of successive instructions is a function of the nature of the elements of the flow. In effect this result indicates how the flow moves as a result of the concatenation of successive instructions T_1 and T_2.

B.7.1 Elements of Transient Flow

In order to avoid losing information, there must be no dead time between the two successive instructions T_1 and T_2. The concept of dead time is evaluated as a function of the life-span of the transient elements and of their speed of propagation, the dead time being a function of the elements of flow under consideration. The result of the two successive instructions T_1 and T_2 is given by

$$(T_1 T_2)^R = T_1 \% \times T_2 \% + T_2 \%$$

In fact a 1 in position (i, j) of $(T_1 T_2)^R$ indicates that either T_2 has allowed a path from i to j; or there is a vertex k such that T_1 has first permitted the path from i to k, then the flow element which has arrived at k has been taken up by T_2 and transmitted to j. It is assumed that the flow elements traversed by T_1 but not taken by T_2 are lost.

B.7.2 Network with Indestructible Flow

There are three types of path

    (a) paths established by T_1 alone, given by $T_1 \%$;
    (b) paths established by T_2 alone, given by $T_2 \%$;
    (c) paths involving both T_1 and T_2 giving

$$(T_1 T_2)^R = (T_1 \% + T_2 \%)\%$$

B.7.3 Network with Tagging Flow

First we shall discuss the result of an instruction.

    Given a path $1 \to 2 \to 3 \to 4 \to 5 \to \ldots \to j$, the result of the instruction which establishes this path is that the vertices $2,3,4,5,\ldots j$ are set to the value of the element that left vertex 1. In $\hat{T}$ only the rows of vertices that are not the first vertex in a path must be removed, that is, every row j of $\hat{T}$ that is non-null in T must be cancelled. Thus T^R is not given by $T\%$ but by

$$T \cdot (\overline{U \times T})$$

The result of two successive instructions T_1 and T_2.
If T_1 and T_2 involve entirely different vertices, the result of $(T_1 T_2)$ is

then $T_1{}^R + T_2{}^R$, otherwise account must be taken of those vertices overlapped by T_2 and the paths of T_1 which are continued by T_2.

B.8 Subgraphs and Sub-instructions

The construction of a subgraph involved the suppression of certain elements of the matrix associated with the graph (the corresponding rows and columns representing suppressed vertices). The same operation on an instruction will be said to generate a sub-instruction.

B.9 Macrograph of a Graph

The macrograph or reduction of graph G is the name given to a graph constructed by first suppressing a number of vertices (called intermediary vertices), and then retaining the existing paths between unsuppressed vertices. The macrograph obtained can be a multigraph, but we shall ignore this secondary effect.

The following example (figure B.2) should help to explain this concept.

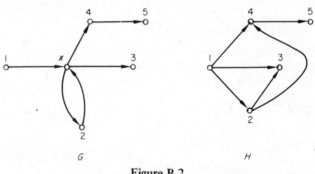

G   H

Figure B.2

B.9.1 Matrix of the Macrograph Obtained by the Suppression of an Intermediary Vertex in Graph G

The suppression of vertex x amounts to replacing all the paths of length 2, of which x is the middle vertex, by new paths of length 1.

Let M_x be the instruction obtained by cancelling all the rows and columns of the matrix M associated with the graph G, except the row and column of x which remain unchanged. A term $m_{ij} = 1$ in $M_x{}^2$ indicates a path of length 2 between i and j, with x at its centre. Then the matrix associated with the macrograph H is obtained by suppressing the row and column of x in $M_x{}^2 + M$.

B.9.2 Relation between a Macrograph and an Instruction

Let T be an instruction. Then the effect of a macrograph on $T^\%$ is to suppress the rows and columns of intermediary vertices.

B.9.3 Significance of the Macrograph

If G represents a situation, a macrograph H of G represents the same situation in a slightly cruder manner, by only attaching importance to certain vertices. For example if G is a road map, H will be the same map simplified by the removal of the smaller towns. Alternatively, if G represents a detailed description of a stored-program computer, H will be an adequate description for the programmer.

B. 10 Micrograph of a Graph G

If G is a macrograph of graph H, then H is a micrograph of G. In other words, if G describes a situation, H describes the same situation in more detail.

Microinstruction for a graph G: this is an instruction of a micrograph specified for G.

Weight of an instruction T, denoted $P(T)$: this is the number of bits of T

Density of a graph G, denoted by $d(G)$

$$d(G) = \frac{\text{number of arcs in } G}{\text{number of vertices in } G} = \frac{P(M)}{|G|}$$

Richness of an instruction T, denoted $R(T)$

$$R(T) = \frac{P(T)}{P(M)} = \frac{P(T)/|G|}{P(M)/|G|} = \frac{d(G_T)}{d(G)}$$

B.11 Analogy between a Computer and a Controlled Graph

It is evident that we can liken a computer to a controlled graph. However, as described in chapter 3 it is important to distinguish between a vertex representing a purely combinational device, across

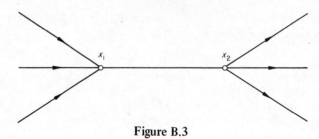

Figure B.3

which information will traverse during an instruction, and a sequential unit like a register, which is not traversed by information in the same way. The method of representing the sequential situation is to use two vertices x_1 and x_2 (figure B.3).

It will further be appreciated that strictly for an instruction T, terms of the form (x_1, x_2) are null. Basically, the computer is a mixed network involving information transmission or information registration. Hence between successive instructions the x_1, x_2 connections are made by an implicit instruction denoted $.

B.11.1 Result of an Instruction

The instruction itself, that is, not the implicit $, does not establish a cycle. In each path specified by the instruction, the intermediary vertices are traversed by the information. These paths are therefore given by $T^\%$, and, taking account of $

$$T^R = T^\% \times \$$$

The contents of the registers will remain unchanged if either no information has been directed to the registers, or a special command has inhibited recording into these registers.

B.11.2 Result of Two Successive Instructions

Let there be two successive instructions T_1 and T_2. The sequence $T_1 T_2$ establishes the following paths

  (a) paths due to T_2 alone, given by $T_2^\% \times \$$,
  (b) paths established by T_1 and taken up by T_2.

These are given by

$$T_1^R \times T_2^R = (T_1^\% \times \$) \times (T_2^\% \times \$)$$

In the paths established by T_1, we must suppress those whose final vertex is overlapped by T_2. Hence, it is necessary to cancel the terms

(i,j) of $T_1{}^R$ if $\exists k$, such that $(k,j) = 1$ in $T_2{}^R$; that is C_j is set to 0 in $T_1{}^R$ whenever $C_j \neq 0$ in $T_2{}^R$. To achieve this, it is sufficient to produce $T_1{}^R \cdot \overline{U \times T_2{}^R}$ which gives

$$(T_1 T_2)^R = T_2{}^R + T_1{}^R \times T_2{}^R + T_1{}^R \cdot U \times T_2{}^R$$

B.12 Concept of Bus in a Controlled Graph

Let us take a graph like that shown in figure B.4. If this is the graph of the connections between 4 registers of a computer, the use of a bus will be as illustrated in figure B.5. In this figure, x is a vertex representing a bidirectional bus. An alternative representation of x is given in figure B.6.

A comparison of graphs G_1 and G_2 shows that there has been a gain in simplicity, and therefore in cost, by replacing G_1 with G_2. (Note that graph G_2 is a macrograph of G_1.) There is however a loss of

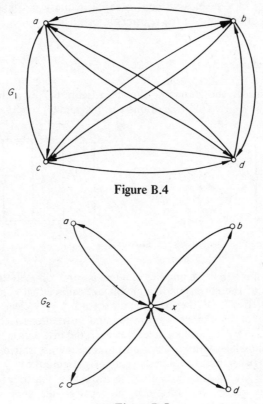

Figure B.4

Figure B.5

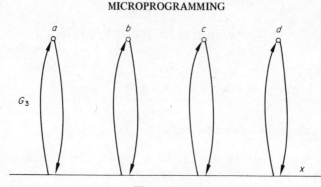

Figure B.6

potentially parallel operation since an instruction of type $(a \rightarrow b,$
$b \rightarrow d)$ for graph G_1 must be replaced by two successive instructions
$(b \rightarrow d)$ then $(a \rightarrow b)$ on G_2. We note also that the instruction $(a \rightarrow b,$
$b \rightarrow c, c \rightarrow d, d \rightarrow a)$ for G_1, is impossible to achieve by a succession of
instructions of G_2 since without a supplementary buffer register, the
content of at least one of the registers is lost.

B.12.1 Replacing a Single Bus with Two Buses

Let us consider the graph G_4 shown in figure B.7, obtained by using
two buses x_1 and x_2 in place of bus x of diagram G_3.

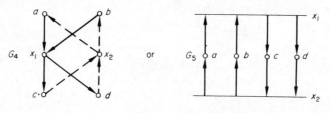

Figure B.7

If we assume that the number of edges is approximately the measure
of the cost of the corresponding circuit, we can see that graph G_4 is of
similar cost to G_2. On the other hand, there is a very clear gain in the
possibilities for simultaneous operation and instructions such as $(a \rightarrow c,$
$d \rightarrow b)$ or $(d \rightarrow a \rightarrow c)$ are possible. However, the instruction $(b \rightarrow a \rightarrow c)$
remains impossible without using an intermediate register or establish-
ing a link between buses x_1 and x_2 (graph G_6, figure B.8).

Note 1   The above considerations show how the transfers macrograph $\rightarrow$ micrograph, or vice versa, take place independently of the
possibilities for simultaneous operation.

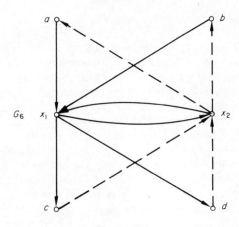

Figure B.8

Note 2 If the number of edges is an approximate measure of the cost of the interconnection circuit, it will be noted that this cost increases with the number of registers. Growth will be factorial for the graph without a bus, and linear in the case where a bus is included.

B.13 Buses and Adjacency Matrices

It is interesting to compare the 'adjacency matrices' corresponding to graphs G_1, G_2 and G_4, as shown in figure B.9.

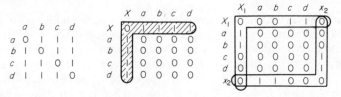

Figure B.9

From figure B.9, it is clear that the transfer from the first to the second, then from the second to the third can take place quite mechanically without considering the corresponding graphs.

The likening of a computer to a controlled graph allows certain questions relevant to the design of the circuits to be formalised. In [1] we were interested in the overlaying of instructions. We have just seen that the use of buses can be represented in terms of graphs. We shall now show how the classic concepts of microinstruction fields [3] are formalised in terms of controlled graphs.

B.13.1 Disconnecting-set Addressing Fields

On graph G_4, $\{x_1 x_2\}$ is a disconnecting set and consideration of the matrix of G_4 leads to a method of finding disconnecting sets. (Note that a disconnecting set is a set such that if the corresponding rows and columns are suppressed, the result is a null matrix.)

The inputs on x_1 and x_2 correspond to the columns x_1 and x_2. The outputs of x_1 and x_2 correspond to the rows x_1 and x_2.

Coding the input and output fields of the two buses corresponds to designating subvectors of these four vectors, taking into account certain characteristics: for example, the columns are limited to subvectors containing at most a single 1. This designation is made by a binary number (generally the number should contain the least number of bits) and the link-gate commands are functions of the bits of this number.

Table B.1

Bus	Number of coding bits		
	Input	Output	Total
A_1	2	3	5
A_2	3	3	6
A_3	3	2	5
F	2	0	2

B.13.2 Designation of an Instruction

Specifying an instruction amounts to designating a submatrix of the connection matrix, again taking into account certain characteristics (for example submatrices not containing more than one 1 per column). Frequently the restriction is that of containing at most 1 per row and per column. Let P be the number designating the submatrix, then P will lie in the range $0 \leqslant P \leqslant 2\Phi$, where the number Φ is generally smaller than that obtained by adding the number of bits necessary to code the input and output fields of each bus separately.

As an example, let us take the matrix shown in figure B.10, which is the matrix of a graph with three buses A_1, A_2 and A_3 with a directed link to vertex F from the vertices D, E and G.

To calculate the total number of possible sub-matrices, the number of connections provided by each bus will be evaluated. This is done by forming the product of number of 1s in the column of the bus with the number of 1s in its row, and adding 1 to allow for the case where the bus is unused.

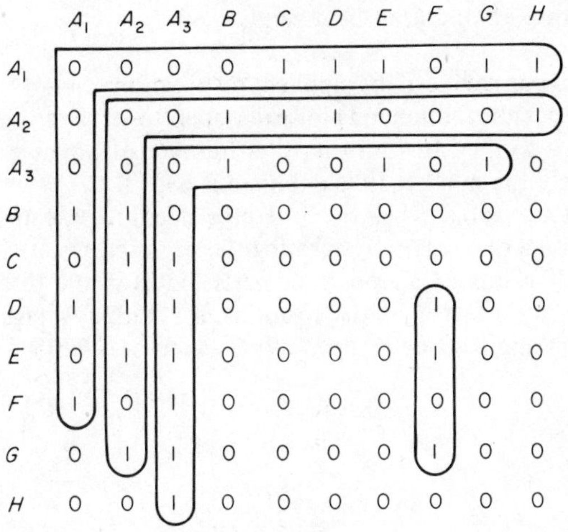

Figure B.10

Subsequently the numbers relating to each bus are multiplied together, though this calculation is not strictly rigorous in cases where inter-bus links are being considered.

In the matrix of figure B.10, the calculation gives

Bus A_1 $3 \times 5 + 1 = 16$

Bus A_2 $5 \times 4 + 1 = 21$

Bus A_3 $6 \times 3 + 1 = 19$

Vertex F $3 \times 1 + 1 = 4$

Total number of possibilities: $16 \times 21 \times 19 \times 4 = 16 \times 399 \times 4$, codable with 15 bits. Usual coding by fields would have led to the situation shown in table B.1 giving a total of 18 bits. The first method therefore enables a saving of three bits to be made, while preserving the independence of the fields. However, the coding in the latter case becomes more complex and so does that of the twenty-nine link commands (equal to the number of 1s in the matrix).

The description of the links to be made should ideally be carried out by automatic calculation. In particular, this calculation re-emphasises the acuteness of the problem of coding tables of boolean functions, and the decomposition and synthesis of these functions, as encountered in microprogramming.

Note In order to determine the sub-instructions, it is not strictly necessary to consider the connection matrix; the very similar matrix of the maximal instruction can be used as an alternative.

B.14 The case of Operator Commands

The same approach can be applied to operator commands: first the number of possible commands for each operator is determined and then a product is formed to find the total number of possible instructions. Subsequently the number thus obtained is coded.

At a more global level the operator and link commands may be considered together, again by forming the product.

Note If a bus or an operator participates in the total number of possibilities by a factor of the form 2^h, it is an advantage not to take into account and to code it separately by means of h bits $X_1 X_2 \ldots X_h$.

References and Bibliography

1. M. V. WILKES, The best way to design an automatic calculation machine. Manchester University Computer Inaugural Conference, 16, 1951
2. N. WIRTH, Microprogramming. Course CS 231 given in 1966—7 at the University of Stanford, California
3. S. G. TUCKER, Microprogram control for System/360. *IBM Systems Journal*, 6, no. 4, 1967 22—41
4. G. BOULAYE, *Logique et organes des calculatrices numériques*. Dunod, Paris, 1970, 277—312
5. R. F. ROSIN, Contemporary Concepts of Microprogramming and Emulation. *Comput. Surv.*, 1 (1969), 197—212
6. H. A. WEBER, Microprogrammed Implementation of EULER on IBM 360-30. *Communs Ass. comput. Mech.*, 10 (1967), 549—58
7. G. HOFF, Design of Microprogrammed Control for General Purpose Processors. See ref. 15, pp. 203—230
8. J. K. ILIFFE and J. MAY, Design of an Emulator for Computer Systems Research. See ref. 15, 281—306
9. L. L. ROKOCSI, Microprogramming the MLP-900 as a Fourth Generation Computer System. See ref. 15, 329—40
10. L. L. RAKOCSI, *B-1700 Systems Reference Manual*, Burroughs Corporation, Detroit, 1972
11. J. K. ILIFFE, *Basic Machine Principles*, 2nd Edition. Macdonald, London, 1972
12. R. F. ROSIN, G. FRIEDER and R. H. ECKHOUSE, An Environment for Research in Microprogramming and Emulation. See ref. 15, 341—96
13. B. A. WICHMAN, Basic Statement Times for Algol 60. NAC 15 (1972), National Physical Laboratory, Teddington
14. A. HASSITT, J. W. LAGESCHULTE and L. E. LYON, Implementation of a High Level Language Machine. *Proc. Ass. Comput. Mach.* SIGMICRO 4th Annual Workshop on Microprogramming (1971)
15 G. BOULAYE and J. MERMET, *Microprogramming. Proceedings of the International Advanced Summer Institute (1972)* Hermann, Paris, 1972
16. G. BOULAYE, Graphes contrôlés et Instructions. *R.I.R.O.*, B-2, 1971
17. S. S. HUSSON, *Microprogramming — Principles and Practice*. Prentice-Hall, Englewood Cliffs, N.J., 1970. For an account of Emulation, see section 3.3
18 W. EILNER, Memory Utilization. Microprogramming environment on the Burroughs 1700. Fall Joint Computer Conference Proceedings, 1972
19. J. ILIFFE, Cours, Alpe d'Huez, December 1972
20. S. G. TUCKER, Emulation of large systems. *Communs. Ass. comput. Mach.*, December 1965, 753—61

Index